A. E Ward

The Sportsman's Guide to Kashmir and Ladak

A. E Ward

The Sportsman's Guide to Kashmir and Ladak

ISBN/EAN: 9783744760683

Printed in Europe, USA, Canada, Australia, Japan

Cover: Foto ©Andreas Hilbeck / pixelio.de

More available books at **www.hansebooks.com**

THE
SPORTSMAN'S GUIDE

TO

KASHMIR & LADAK, &c.,

BY

A. E. WARD,

BENGAL STAFF CORPS.

———◆———

REPRODUCED WITH ADDITIONS FROM LETTERS WHICH
APPEARED IN THE "ASIAN."

———◆———

SECOND AND REVISED EDITION.

———◆———

Calcutta:

PUBLISHED BY THE CALCUTTA CENTRAL PRESS CO., LD.,
5, COUNCIL HOUSE STREET.

1883.

PREFACE.

THESE lines are written in the hope that, after their perusal, the visitor to "The Vale," or to other parts of the Himalayas, may not feel himself so entirely at the mercy of his shikari, who too often consults his own comfort, and visits spots where he and the villagers can play into one another's hands, and neglects localities where the best bags are to be obtained.

The object, therefore, is not to write a book of adventures, but to give accurate measurements, the names of the best shooting grounds, and such hints as are likely to prove useful to the inexperienced traveller in the hills and ravines of the Himalayas, and amongst the sterile mountains and plains of Ladak and Middle Thibet.

No attempt has been made to compile a scientific treatise. A book of this description would only bore the general reader, and a work now in the Press, by Mr. Sterndale, gives much information to the naturalist. A guide to the various shooting grounds does not exist, and the want of it is often keenly felt.

It is quite impossible for one traveller to have an intimate knowledge of the vast field for shooting which is included in the mountains of Hindustan and Thibet. The author acknowledges with gratitude the assistance given to him by several friends; and more especially to a gentleman who has resided in Kashmir for the last fifteen years, his sincere thanks are due.

At times the reader will find it difficult to trace the various localities on the maps. In order to lessen this evil the author has done his best to refer to some fairly well-known village or river, in the vicinity of the ground he may be describing, and has added in the new Edition a few maps.

It is hoped that the object of the skeleton maps, now added, may not be misunderstood. They are little more than clues to the localities mentioned in the book, and will, it is hoped, serve to render the description of the various routes plainer.

They are added at the request of several friends who have complained of the difficulty they have experienced in tracing out the shooting grounds referred to in these pages.

The only maps which are of any real use are those on the scale of one inch to four miles. They are to be obtained from Messrs. Thacker, Spink & Co., of Calcutta. In England almost any description of bound map can be purchased at 457, Strand, but it is far preferable to buy the ordinary quarter sheets, for a big map is difficult to manipulate, and in a high wind, and on a small camp table, it is sufficiently aggravating to try the temper of the most amiable of mankind.

All the measurements given have been made by the author, unless it is particularly noted to the contrary. By far the greater number of places have been visited by him, and it is believed that all information so kindly afforded to him is the result of *recent* experiences.

It will, therefore, be understood that this is a sportsman's and not a naturalist's book, and what success may have attended the author in his various wanderings can be confidently expected by any one possessing the love of sport, and that most valuable of gifts—a good constitution. At one time it was intended to have added a list of the largest measurements of horns on record, but this idea has been abandoned; for it appears that a gentleman of great experience is devoting himself to this undertaking.

CHAPTER I.

The Shikaris of Kashmir and of Ladak—The cost of a shooting excursion—The decrease of game—Seasons for shooting.

In Kashmir there exist two or three hundred men who call themselves shikaris, but there are not two dozen who are worthy of the name. In no other part of India have I come across such an arrant collection of impostors. I quote from a letter of mine which the Editor of the *Asian* was kind enough to comment upon in one of his leading articles.

"As a rule the Kashmiri is a good walker and is keen sighted ; but only the very best of the fraternity are of any use after Ibex and Markhor. I would certainly not advise any one to go after Ibex or Markhor without the aid of the natives of the country ; but I do deprecate the employment of the host of followers it is the custom to entertain. Most people, when they arrive in Kashmir, engage a shikari; if possible they employ a ·man who has been recommended to them, but failing this, they have to fall back on any one who has a parcel of recommendations. Well and good, this is to a great extent unavoidable ; but what follows ?

"The shikari must, he says, have an assistant shikari; then there must be a man to carry luncheon, and a certain staff of coolies. One and all of this gathering do their best not to do any work. They are hangers-on of that grand gentleman, the Kashmiri shikari, and in return for employment found, they work for him in his village during the winter months. This is not all. In addition to wages ; rice, dal, and salt have to be supplied, and not unfrequently ghee, sheep and even tobacco or snuff are demanded. Custom has decreed that twenty rupees and food are the head shikari's wages, and now it is too late to alter it ; but why engage an assistant on twelve, and a luncheon coolie on seven ?

"Insist on the shikari carrying a rifle, and doing his own scouting ; give him, when necessary, the aid of a local man who can carry the luncheon-basket and a spare gun ; keep up a staff of coolies to carry baggage and to collect wood, but give them to understand that you are their master, and that the shikari is your servant, and the result will be that, after a little trouble at first, you will have a much more enjoyable trip, and, in all probability, will return with a better bag of game."

Amongst a large gang of followers you are certain to be kept in the dark as to all movements, and you will be led about here and there, scarcely knowing where you are bound for.

The better class of shikaris can and will work in the hope of getting a reward or a recommendation to some friend of the sportsman who may take him into service during the coming season.

When a sportsman has had some experience in Kashmir, and become conversant with the ways of the country, he may well dispense with the "professional," and fall back on the local talent of each ravine he visits. He will then only require the services of two good coolies, instead of shikaris and their followers. They will bring wood for the campfire, water to the cook-house, and carry the rifles on the march. Any one who shoots for the pleasure of the thing will value a pair of horns, which he has obtained without aid, far more than another head, towards getting which he has done nothing more than pull the trigger.

The men who in Ladak follow the trade of "professional shikari" are few and far between. They are not at all keen on taking service, and are much more likely to deny the existence of game than to invent stories which may lead the visitor to give them employment. They are naturally lazy, obstructive, and obstinate, but some are exceptions to the rule, and make good servants. In Lahoul and Spiti the shikaris are generally honest, moderate in their demands, and fairly anxious to please, but are greatly wanting in enterprise. In Ghurwal, Bussahir and in the estates of the various petty rajas in the neighbour-hood of our north-west sanitaria, they are very different to the Kashmir impostors, and, as a rule, are reliable and hard-working.

Very few of the Himalayan shikaris are good trackers, and none can be compared with the men of the wild tribes of the Central Provinces.

Since the habit of employing so many retainers has come into vogue, the cost of shooting in Kashmir has been greatly increased. Still it is the country for men who cannot afford to expend large sums on sport. For outfit it is impossible to fix any figure, but I should strongly recommend a few things to be selected.

Provide your tent with net-work pockets, and have an outer fly covered with khaki drill, for a white tent in a Thibetan nullah can be seen for miles by the game.

The servants' tents are best made of brown blankets thrown over a male bamboo ridge pole; the ridge to be supported on a couple of forked sticks which can be used as walking sticks by the coolies.

Clothing.—Puttoo suits made in Srinuggar, fur-lined gloves, flannel shirts, a Cardigan jacket with sleeves, broad-soled boots.

Cooking Utensils.—Block tin cooking pots.

Etceteras.—Butcher's skinning knives, shoemaker's sewing implements, packing needles, housewife and worsted for darning socks, a telescope, binoculars, flint and steel.

For a battery.—I can only say what I myself prefer in the hills, and that is D. B. C. F. '500 bore Express by Henry, charge 5¾ drachms, and a 12-bore gun.

For Stores.—Cocoa, tea, oatmeal, jams. For Thibet add Normandy butter, Swiss milk, and corned beef, dried fruits and vegetables.

The annexed table of expenses should be sufficient for any one who cares to go to the more remote ravines, and thus give himself the best chance of getting good trophies :—

Carriage of one small tent and personal baggage 4 men at Rs. 6			= Rs. 24
„ „ cook house tent, utensils, &c. ... 2 „ „ „			= „ 12
„ „ stores ... ... 2 „ „ „			= „ 12
Gun *cases* and ammunition ... ... 1 „ „ „			= „ 6
Servants' baggage ... ... 1 „ „ „			= „ 6
Cook's pay, Rs. 10 ; Shikari, Rs. 20 ; Two coolies, Rs. 10			= „ 40
Food for self, Rs. 20 ; for 4 servants, Rs. 15 ...			= „ 35
Runners to Srinaggar and payment of local shikaris, &c.			= „ 30
		TOTAL RS.	... 165

To this must be added, in many cases, the carriage of food for the servants. The cost of this depends on the distance from the nearest depôt for supplies ; but it should not swell the total beyond Rs. 200. Wines and stores can be made to amount to any sum, and if much is required, the item "carriage" will be materially increased. It may be objected that I have supposed the traveller to move his camp daily ; but, although he will probably halt at least half his time, it will be found necessary to engage the men permanently as he will be past the line of villages.

A list of the authorized rates is appended :—

			Rs. As. P.
Coolie by the day halting	...	...	... 0 2 0
„ per march ...	...	...	... 0 4 0
Dandy bearer	...	...	... 0 6 0
Baggage pony per march	...	...	... 0 8 0
Riding „ „ „	...	...	... 1 0 0

Custom has settled :—

Head shikari ...	...	Rs. 20 and food per mensem.	
Assistant „ ...	... about	„ 10 „ „	
Tiffin coolie ...	... „	„ 7 „ „	
Baggage „ ...	... „	„ 5 „ „	

A coolie employed in the vicinity of his own village gets Rs. 6 per mensem and no food. Thus, when the sportsman goes up the Krishnye, the coolies are hired at the warm springs, and get this rate of pay.

In Thibet, Yak hire is cheap; the drivers bring their own food and provide carriage for it. The ordinary charge per Yak is Rs. 8 to Rs. 12 a month.

In other portions of the Himalayas rates vary so much that no exact figures can be given, but of one thing I feel certain, that, omitting the cost of wines or spirits, any one should be able to march from end to end of the Himalayas for Rs. 300 per mensem, and should be able to wander all over Kashmir for a much lower sum.

I have no belief in being stingy, and in making oneself unnecessarily uncomfortable ; but it is often more trouble to take luxuries than to do without them.

The decrease of game is chiefly due to shooting out of season, to the use of nets and nooses, and other unfair means for killing game.

Fair shooting does not do much harm ; and, if the sportsman also fires at all vermin he sees, the chances are that in the long run he does more good than harm. Every leopard, wolf, or wild dog *met* with is as a rule fired at ; but foxes, pine martens, weasels, and birds of prey are seldom interfered with. The purchasers of game are much more to be blamed than the native who traps it during the breeding season.

The question is so often asked: " When shall I take leave so as to ensure getting sport ?" This table of seasons may aid towards a reply :—

Himalayas within the action of the monsoon.

March, April, and May, and half of June are the best months for large game.

Half June, July, and August are generally so rainy that no sport is to be got.

In September, October and November the weather is, as a rule, perfect, but the vegetation is rank. These are the months for pheasant-shooting.

December, January, and February are cold ; and at any elevation over 7,000 feet there is too much snow.

The Himalayas beyond the action of the monsoon, in which parts of Kashmir may be included, can be visited comfortably during the whole year unless the snow bars the way.
For Kashmir and Ladak.

January and February, if the snow is deep, are good for stag-shooting.

March is a sure time to get the stags, for they are low down grazing on the green grass.

The latter half of April, the whole of May, and part of June is *the time* for Ibex and Markhor.

From June 15th to September 15th very little can be done in Kashmir ; the game can wander over all the mountain tops which are then free from snow. The bears are out of fur, and their coats valueless. These are the months for Thibet.

September 15th to November 1st the barasingh are calling and are returning from their summer retreats. The bears are getting worth shooting, and the chikore are to be found in the lower hills.

November and December. There is one great drawback to shooting during these two months; the grass is dry, noisy, and slippery, but November can advantageously be spent after red bears or after the Kashmir Markhor. In December the grass is dangerously slippery, and the bears are hibernating. An early snowfall will however cure the first evil, and will also cause the stags to descend. The wild fowl are numerous, but are difficult to approach; they are continually harassed by the boatmen, and will not allow a boat to get near them.

CHAPTER II.

Routes to Leh, &c.—A few shooting routes.

In Dr. Ince's Handbook of Kashmir will be found details of the authorized routes into the valley.

They are:—

1. *Via*   Goojerat and the Pir Panjal.
2.   „   Rawal Pindi and Murree.
3.   „   Peshawur and Hazara.
4.   „   Goojerat and Poonch.

From Srinaggar to Leh the route is slightly altered.

No.	STAGE.	MILES.	SUPPLIES.	REMARKS.
1.	Gunderbal	14	Good	By boat or by road.
2.	Kangaum	11	„	
3.	Goond	14	Doubtful	House.
4.	Gugangair	10	None.	
5.	Soonamurg	9	Only milk.	
6.	Baltal	10	None	Huts.
7.	Mataiyan	15	„	Cross Zogila. Matahoy is half way. Huts, but very dirty.
8.	Dras	15	Good	Large house.
9.	Tashgaum	16	Fair	Serai.
10.	Kargil	23	Good	House. Pass Changaum at 16 miles. Supplies only obtainable by previous notice. Pay for 1½ stages.
11.	Shergol	20	Fair	Serai.
12.	Kurbo	19	„	„ Pass Moolbekh.
13.	Lama Yuru	16	Good	„ Lay in supplies if going by Wanla.
14.	Snurla	20	Fair.	
15.	Saspul	20	„	Serai.
16.	Snemo	15	„	„
17.	Leh	18	Good	Bungalow.

Leh to Changchenmo.

1.	Runbeer Bagh. Tikzay	10	Fair.	
2.	Chimray	15	Good	Last place where wheat flour is got.
3.	Zingral	8	None	Serai under the pass. No fuel. Camp about 16,000.
4.	Durgu	17	„	Cross Changla, start early.
5.	Tankse	5	Fair	House and Garden. Last chance of supplies.
6.	Muglib	9	None.	
7.	Tsearh Tso	5	„	Bhurrel to right and left.
8.	Phobrang or Chuggra.	12 to 14	„	Pass Lukung.

No.	STAGE.	MILES.	SUPPLIES.	REMARKS.
9.	Foot of Marsemik	6 to 8	None	Cross Pass.
10.	Panglung or Rimdi Guinlay.	8 to 10	„	„
11.	Pamzal	8	„	Changchenmo valley, fuel.
12.	Kyam	8	„	Fuel.

There is an alternative route from Zingral over Kayla. Halt at Kay Tso after crossing the Pass ; next day go to Tankse.

From Tankse there is a route to Mirpa Tso and the Thatoola ; instead of going to Muglib cross the river, and go up the back of the ranges which bound the Pangong to the south, and then to get to Changchenmo come round the ranges, and march along the borders of the lake by man to Lukung.

[See map of Changchenmo.]

Route from Srinaggar to Wardwan.

No.	STAGE.	MILES.	SUPPLIES.	REMARKS.
1.	Kanbal	...	Good	By boat.
2.	Changus	7	„	Early in the year ask at Kanbal if store is open. Lay in rice and salt for the whole trip.
3.	Nowboog	12	Only milk and fowls.	
4.	Foot of Murgan	7	None.	
5.	Over Pass	18	Fowls and milk	Cross Murgan.
6.	Gweenye	10	None	Camp at entrance of nullah.
7.	Maru	14	Fowls and sheep.	Capital of Wardwan.

From Maru to Krishnye.

No.	STAGE.	MILES.	SUPPLIES.	REMARKS.
1.	Warm Springs	10	Fowls and sheep	Engage coolies by month.
2.	Furriabad	13	None	Pass Metwan, the east village.
3.	Opposite Dichnye	4		
4.	Tekh Murg	...		
5.	Mundik Sir	...	These are all shooting marches. There is a cave at Tekh Murg and stones for shelter in all, but Mundik Sir. Distances, 2 to 5 miles.	
6.	Keyl Gye	...		
7.	Ladhi Hoie	...		
8.	Turring Hoie	...		

The Zaisnye branches off at Furriabad.

The Birbalnve joins the main nullah between the "Warm Springs" and Furriabad.

From Srinaggar there are alternative routes to Astor and Boonji. These places can be reached by the direct road or by going over the Zogila, and then along the Leh road ; and from Changaum by working across to Iskardo, Rondu, &c.

Direct Routes—Srinaggar to Astor.

No.	STAGE.	MILES.	SUPPLIES.	REMARKS.
1.	Bandipoor	0	Good ...	By boat over the Woolar; take coolies to Gurais.
2.	Kralpoora	5	Doubtful.	
3.	Tragbal	6	None.	
4.	Zudkoosoo	9	„ ...	Cross Rajdiangan Pass.
5.	Kanzelwan	7	„	
6.	Goorais	8	Milk, &c. ...	Take on coolies to Dars and all supplies.
7.	Bangla	10	None.	
8.	Mapunun	6	„	
9.	Minimurg	4	„	
10.	Boozil	5	„	
11.	Sirdar-ki Koti	9	„	
12.	Dars	8	„ ...	Take on coolies to Astor.
13.	Godhai	10	„	
14.	Margam	8	„	
15.	Astor	12	Fair.	
16.	Duskin	14	None.	
17.	Dognee	12	„	
18.	Ramghat	10	„	
19.	Boonji	13	Doubtful.	

or at march 7 go to (1), Lishat, 7 miles; (2), Loyen Harda, 16 miles; (3), Marmeri, &c. See next route. Or from—

No.	STAGE.	MILES.	SUPPLIES.	REMARKS.
5.	Kanzelwan to			
6.	Tharbut	9	None.	
7.	Gugai Pass	10	„ ...	Up Chota Gugai.
8.	Loyen Harda	12	„ ...	Cross Pass.
9.	Marmeri	12	„	
10.	Chongam	14	„	
11.	Goorekeet	12	„	
12.	Astor	7	Fair.	

The first of these routes, over the Darikom pass, and *via* Boozil, is the easiest. It is open in April.

The second is difficult, and is open in May. This route is by Lishat and the Kamri Pass. The third is by Gagai and the Gagai pass, and is the most difficult of the three.

I am informed that there is a route from Foolmai going to the Rattu plain *via* Mir Mullick.

The generality of visitors arrive in Kashmir, about 25th April, but some sportsmen, who come from England, often have a large amount of spare time on their hands, and have not to be back by any fixed date. To them I would recommend the following routes:—

Secure as soon as possible one of the Soroo "Ibex Nullahs;" endeavour to be on the ground by the first week in April. Soroo can be reached from Srinaggar either by crossing the Zogila Pass, and then turning off to the right from Dras, or by the Wardwan route. The length of time taken on the road depends on a man's walking powers. Early in the season there will be no occasion to hurry, so I will suppose he marches leisurely. By boat he will reach Kanbal bridge in two days, and can then walk on seven miles to Changus village. Here he will get supplies of rice and salt which must suffice to carry him on to Soroo. From Changus it is an easy march to Nowboog; the third march is to any spot under the Murgan Pass; the fourth is over the pass. Then it is a long march to Sooknis; and from there he will require three to five days, according to what nullah he selects. At Soroo flour is easily obtained, and is the depôt from which he will draw future supplies (Map of Liddar Valley, &c., Chap. XII).

After having secured some Ibex heads, cross the glaciers, and hit off the Ladak road near Lama-Yuru Then march down to Leh; from there visit the Changchenmo, and utilize the months of July and August in the pursuit of Ovis Ammon, Burhel and Antelope. On the way back have a look at some of the haunts of the Sharpoo, and get into Kashmir in time for the stag-shooting. After the stags have ceased calling, it is a good plan to visit the grazing grounds where the sheep have been folded during the summer, and pick up one or two red bears. When leaving the valley, go out either by the Poonch route, taking the Sallar "Markhor ground" on the way, or else stay a few days in the Kaj-uag hills, and leave by Murree. (Map of Kajnag, Chapter IV).

Or, if of a more adventurous turn, the following programme might be suitable:—

Cross the Zogila Pass before the heavy snow sets in. This generally can be done as late as December 1st; then march steadily along the Ladak road to Lama-Yuru. When there, shoot Sharpoo, for these animals come down close to the village during the winter months. Work the whole of the ground between Lama-Yuru and the Hinjo Pass. The road to Hinjo lies through Waula; the distance is about 20 miles to the foot of the pass. Do not cross this pass, for there might be difficulty in getting on, or back again! Pay particular attention to the heights above Wanla for Ibex, and to the country south of the Waula gorge for Burhel. By January 20th, the traveller can return to Lama-Yuru, and then visit the Ibex nullahs of Kulsi and Basgo, and the plains that are frequented by Sharpoo. Leh will be the next place to visit; and to refit will probably take a few days. Leaving Leh in March, work up the Indus to Hanle, taking the Ovis Ammon ground near Gya and Tiri *en route;* in June, after shooting the Thibet ravine deer near the Tso-Morari lake, turn up northwards and march along the Pangong lake to Changchenmo. Give a few days to the Antelope; return by Tankse to Leh; then work along the Kashmir road to Changaum (see route to Leh), and from there take the road to Iskardo, and visit the Markhor ground; then

2

return to the valley for stags, and go out by the Murree or
Poonch routes, and the habitat of all the different kinds of
Kashmir, Ladak or Thibetan game will have been visited. If
it is found that the Zogila Pass is likely to remain open later
than December 1st, it would be better to delay, as the
time spent between Lama-Yuru and Leh might hang heavily
on hand.

Most men have only six months at their disposal; out of
this time one month is necessarily lost in travelling to and from
the valley of Kashmir. During one expedition of this
duration, it is hopeless to expect to obtain shots at every kind
of hill game, and by attempting too much, it not unfrequently
happens that the sportsman ruins his chances of doing well
after any one of the various animals. If a man reaches
Kashmir in April, my advice to him would be, leave Srinaggar
as quickly as can be arranged, make up his mind what
specimens he wishes to secure, and remember that it is almost
impossible to make sure of more than three or four varieties.

If the selection is Ibex, Astor, Markhor, and Oorin
(Sharpoo), his route is evidently fixed; he must go to the Astor
side (Map, Chap. IV). On his way back he may pick up a
stag or two on the high ground above Bandipoora, say, in Gugai.
He will in all probability have secured a few Bears and Musk
Deer; but his mind should be set on Ibex and Markhor. If,
on the other hand, he wishes to get Ibex and the game of
Thibet, he must follow one of the routes already described.
The chances of getting red Bears are small, for time will not
allow of his remaining to try after either the Bears or Kashmir
Markhor. In fact, it is possible that he might prefer to return
from Haule by the Simla route.

If a combination of shooting and society is wished for, what
is pleasanter than to follow the Ibex until June, then to visit
Gulmurg, and after the season is over try for the Barasingh.

It hink Soonamurg, the second hill station of Kashmir, is a much
prettier place than Gulmurg, but it is further from Srinaggar,
and seems of late years to have been deserted, chiefly, I fancy,
owing to the want of supplies. Gulmurg is only two marches
from the capital, whereas Soonamurg is five.

To employ six months' leave if Astor or Ladak are visited
is very simple, but the difficulty of settling where to go for
three months is great, for most of the ground near the valley
is greatly shot over.

Three months leave means but two months after game; and
I would not advise any one to spend their hard-earned privi-
lege leave in Kashmir unless they can so time it as to arrive in
Srinaggar by April 1st or else by September 1st.

In the first case, the arriver on April 1st will, in all likeli-
hood, have his choice of the Wardwan and Soroo Ibex nullahs,

and by turning his attention to only Ibex and red Bears he should do well. On September 1st there will be time to secure a good locality for stags, and before leaving, for getting a few Bears, or possibly a Markhor.

If fate decreed that leave could not be obtained so as to arrive before May 1st, I should strongly recommend the Pir Panjal, for all the good ground in the Wardwan and elsewhere would be occupied.

Shorter leave than three months would point to the Pir, or to the Kaj-nag only, and would, in all probability, result in a complete failure. There are many spots near our hill sanataria that could be visited on sixty days' leave, but I do not propose to touch on them here. Later on, when pointing out the favorite resorts of some varieties of game, I will mention a few places which may prove attractive to those sportsmen who have but a short spell of liberty on hand.

The routes I have given naturally admit of great variation. Leh can be reached by following the Zaskar river to its junction with the Indus. There is also a route from the Krishnye which leads into Ladak. There is a road to Sooknis from the Liddar valley; and many other bye-paths are open. (Map, Chapter XII).

In the preceding directions I have supposed Srinaggar to be the base of operations, but it is by no means necessary that this should be adhered to. A start can be made from any of the North-West or Punjab Hill Stations, and by working through the Ibex ground in Spiti; through the vicinity of the Tso-Morari lake and Hanle in pursuit of Ovis Ammon, Burhel and Goa a good bag might be made. If preferred, instead of going from Hanle northwards to the Indus, there is nothing to prevent the traveller from passing through the Rukshu country over the Tagalang pass, and so on to Leh vid Gya and Miru. The middle of May would be early enough to start on this trip.

CHAPTER III.

Himalayan game—Fur producers—Pheasants, &c.

IN the dominions of the Maharaja of Kashmir a great variety of game is to be found—in fact specimens of almost every kind of Himalayan trophies can be obtained.

The goats are represented by two varieties of Markhor—the Ibex and the Ther. The capricorns or antelope goats include the Serow and the Goral.

The sheep are three in number—the Ovis Ammon, Ovis Vignei, with one or two closely allied varieties, and the Burhel. The Deer family have the Kashmir Stag, the Musk Deer, and the Barking Deer.

Then follow the Antelope and Ravine Deer of Thibet.

The Yak representing the cattle.

The Kyang or Wild Ass of Thibet.

The red and black Bears in Kashmir and parts of Ladak.

The cat tribe consists of the Leopard, the Ounce, the Thibet Lynx, and one or two unimportant Jungle Cats.

The dogs include two or more species of wolves, and the wild dog.

Pigs are found in some parts, and at one time were common in the Liddar, Sindh, &c.

The gigantic *Ovis polii* and *O. karelini,* the Central Asian antelope Gutturosa, are not met with on ground that can, under ordinary circumstances, be visited by the English sportsman; but the horns can sometimes be purchased from traders.

The Maral or Maralbashi stag is another trophy which must be bought. The horns are sold in the Yarkand bazar.

The Sambhur takes the place of the Barasingh or Kashmir Stag in our British possessions.

The Oorial or Hourian of the Salt Range must be mentioned, for although it is not found in the countries in which we are now chiefly concerned, it often forms an item in the game list of the visitor to the valley, who has the time and inclination to stop at Jhelum.

Some of the fur-producing animals are greatly in request. The marmot, the hill fox, the jackal, a lynx-like wild cat, three or four varieties of flying squirrel, including an almost black variety from the Pir Panjal, an excessively handsome little marten, from Tilail, the common pine marten, and a few weasels are those generally to be purchased. Otter skins are rarely to be bought, and are expensive.

Messrs. Hume and Marshall's exhaustive treatise on the game birds of India gives a long list of bill pheasants, partridges, &c., so that but few remarks are necessary.

The monaul, the koklass, the kaleege, the ram chikore, and the common chikore are in places fairly common in Kashmir.

Wild fowls are numerous on the various lakes.

Woodcock are to be found.

Snipe are found in Kashmir.

Sandgrouse in Thibet.

The cheer pheasant, black partridges, wood partridges and other game birds abound in some of our own Himalayas.

The so-called Argus of sportsmen is very rare in Kashmir, but is more plentiful in Chumba and near Kishtwar.

Hares are common in many places, but are not found in Kashmir proper.

As I intend to devote one chapter to small game shooting, I do not think it necessary to go into any great details here, for but few people care to follow birds in Kashmir.

CHAPTER IV.

THE MARKHOR (*Capra megaceros* and *Capra falconeri*).

*In Kashmir, Markhor; Raché of Ladak; and also called in Astor
the Boom.*

THIS splendid wild goat is far more difficult to obtain than the
Ibex, and is consequently more highly prized. On the shooting
grounds which are open to the European sportsmen, fine old
bucks are seldom met with, and rarely a good trophy is obtained.
A pair of massive horns, over 50 inches in length, is worth
many long days of really hard work. In fact an old male
Markhor's head from the Pir Panjal, from the Astor mountains,
from Sheik Budin, or from any locality, and of whatever
variety, is a trophy worth the most artistic setting up, and
when set up, a place of honour on the wall of the room or
hall. (Index map).

Some of the heads from the Pir Panjal are very handsome;
they have fine massive sweeping curves, and occasionally three
complete spirals. I have lately seen a pair 47 inches in length,
and doubtless larger do exist. Adams mentions obtaining one
of 48½ inches.

In the Kaj-nag and Shamshibri ranges very good heads are
still to be obtained, but they vary much in appearance and
thickness. Annexed are the measurements of two pairs of
horns shot in the same stalk; both these bucks were very old
ones, the teeth being worn away; in fact some were missing.
It will be seen at a glance what different appearances these
horns presented :—

Length along the curve.	Girth.	Divergency at tips.	No. of spirals.
53 inches ...	9½ inches	... 26 inches	...	2¼
43 ,, ...	11 ,,	... 31 ,,	...	2½

The longer of the two reminded me forcibly of the Markhor
from the Sheik Budin hills. The spirals were sharp, but the
horns lacked the roundness of that variety. I have no large
horns from Sheik Budin to measure, nor do I remember having
seen any of great length. A friend, who knew the shooting on
those hills in their palmy days, says that the largest pair he
succeeded in obtaining were 36 inches in length.

From Afghanistan I possess a pair of 35 inches, which are
said to be good specimens, and are the largest I have come
across. They are massive up to the top, round in section, and
afford a striking contrast to the next variety—the Astor, or
Nunga Purbat Markhor.

This animal is larger than its representative in Kashmir proper.
Many stand as much as eleven hands, whereas the largest I

Missing Page

.

KASHMIR AND LADAK, ETC.   15

have seen in other localities barely reached ten and a half
hands. The curves of the horns are bold and flat, the diver-
gency at the tips great, and the massiveness, which is shown to
such advantage by the single twist, leads this variety to be considered by most people the handsomest of the four. Some very
fine specimens have been brought down from the Astor shooting
grounds, amongst them single horns of 63 and 61 inches, and
I have lately measured a head with horns—

Length along curve.	Girth.	Divergency at tips.
52 inches ...	12½ inches ...	43 inches.

I have seen several pairs which had been picked up in the
snow about this size, but unluckily they were all more or less
damaged.

Trophies of this size are rare, and a hard-working sportsman
who wintered on the Gilgit side of the passes in order to
obtain some fine heads, was only successful in getting one good
specimen out of the thirteen he shot. Few men are capable
of doing more than the gentleman I allude to, and rare indeed is
a head with horns much over 50 inches in length.

For localities in the different tracts of country where sport is
likely to be obtained, I begin with the Pir Panjal, and mention
Sallar and Jarginee and the Tosha-Maidan near the Norpal Pass.
The Chotagullee and the Chitapani, these two rivulets join and
form the Posheana river. Beyond the Pir Pass towards the
Koonjenag range, Markhor do not appear to wander. The
suitable season is as soon as the snow is sufficiently melted
to allow of the game being followed. In most years this is
not before the 10th of May.

In the Kaj-nag range, the Kutai nullah, which is marked on
the map, is a first-rate place, and after a mild winter it should be
visited in March. A little later try the Luchipoora nullahs,
viz., the Malangan, the Bawni, the Goojur and Puch. This
last is recommended in the rutting season (which is in December) provided the snow has fallen, if not the grass is so dry,
and the leaves crackle so noisily under the most careful tread,
that stalking is only waste of time. In April the Limbur
nullahs, particularly the two branches of the Khar Kohl, of which
the local names are the Gaumlitter and Metabwyan, are the
resort of large Markhor. With the exception of the Kutai,
these ravines are all small, and do not stand much firing.

For the Shamshibri mountains May is a good month. These
hills lie to the north of Kaj-nag. The Markhor frequents the
ground as far as Teetwal on the Kishenganga river.

In the provinces of Baltistan, Astor, Rondu, and Gilgit there
are wide hunting fields and endless hills and ravines, most of
which hold Markhor and Ibex. To avoid repetition I shall not,
when writing on the Ibex, go over the same ground which I am
now entering upon, but will ask the reader to remember that

fine Ibex are to be got in nearly all the places I am about to mention.

It would far exceed the limits of one chapter if I were to enumerate all the likely spots; and moreover it would be useless, as they could not be traced on the maps. Unfortunately, although the outlines of the various hills and streams are marked, but few places are named. Take up the quarter sheets 27 A. S. E. and 27 A. N. E., and I will endeavour to guide the traveller to the spots I am anxious to point out.

On 27 A. S. E. will be found the Astor river. Marching down the river, Duskin is reached. On the right bank of the river, and opposite to Duskin, is the Ditchell ravine; then comes the Shelterie; then Dutchnar. This last is near the junction of the Astor with the Indus. Sportsmen who have shot over these nullahs during the month of May have nearly always seen good heads of both the wild goats. Between the junction and Boonjie is the nullah of the same name. Now glance up north of Boonjie, the small stream which joins the left bank of the Indus, and on the extreme edge of the map is the Musken. On the same bank, but higher up the river, and next to the Musken, is the Bellachee nullah. The Bellachee and the next ravine, the Bulteree, have their heads amongst the glaciers which lie due east of Boonjie. Close to Bulteree is the Durdoth which enters the Indus at Sapser. The Juchee is a branch of this last ravine.

At last we find a place that is marked on every map—Rondu.

Across the river the range above Rondu holds good Markhor, the best ground being the Achkor stream which joins the Indus due west of Rondu.

Now take up the other map 27 N. E., and use it in conjunction with the S. E. map. At the bend of the Indus stands the small village of Haramosh and the ravine which takes its name. Next to it should be the well known Baralomah; but here I must stop; either the maps, or the joint information of several sportsmen who know the ground is incorrect.

Now look at the Nunga Purbat mountain. The northern slopes are doubtless good ground; but it is not a country over which much travelling can be done, for the inhabitants of Chilas are not renowned for hospitality! In the summer the Dognee and Huttoo Pir might advantageously be wandered over.

Again turn to Boonji. After crossing the Indus, Dumoot and Changroot can be visited, also Monaor and the Shingaigye, and to the west of Gilgit is Kirgah. Here are the extreme borders where it is safe to travel. In fact at the time that I am penning these lines, these shooting grounds are closed. A sheet showing Gilgit and the vicinity is now available, and any one wishing to visit the vicinity should certainly purchase it. The day may come when the Yassein and other tribes

Missing Page

will be less turbulent, so some notes by the late Mr. Hayward
are given.

The reader is perhaps aware that Mr. Hayward was mur-
dered by the tribesmen in 1870 when on his second expedition
to those parts.   He wrote after his first journey : " For big Ibex
and Markhor, the head of the Shingye valley, west of Gilgit
fort, above the village of Bargoo, fourteen miles from Gilgit,
towards Yassein.   Two small nullahs joining Bargoo hold good
Ibex at their heads, near the Boomeril or Booril peak."   A
friend who shot over the Shingye not long since used the
expression : " I saw the biggest Markhor and Ibex in the Himalayas."   Unluckily he was recalled by the British Resident at
Gilgit before he could leave his mark on the game.

The whole of the country described is particularly suitable
for Markhor.   In the winter months they can descend into
lower country, and in the summer, they can wander up to
almost any elevation.   Unlike the Ibex, the Markhor does not
delight in snow, and I think I am correct in stating that the
latter are not found in countries that are not adjacent to low-
lying hills not exceeding 7,500 feet elevation.   From Rondu
to Boonjie the Indus valley varies from about 6,600 to 4,600
feet above the sea.

Markhor are gregarious, and are sometimes met with in very
large herds.   The small males and females may be seen together
at all seasons, but the older bucks often hold aloof from the
main gathering.   In their winter coat of grey they are difficult
to discern, for they often stand motionless amongst the rocks
which are of the same color.   Again, when the under fleece has
been shed, and the animal presents a reddish or brownish hue,
they are still more difficult to see when in the dried-up grass.
When in the forest, none but an experienced eye will find
them out.

The black beard and masses of hair on the neck and breast
add greatly to the beauty of the trophy, and the shikari should
be warned not to cut the throat from ear to ear in the orthodox
fashion, but to leave the full length of neck skin intact.   This
caution is given, for the sportsman is not likely to have many
chances of procuring really fine specimens, and may bitterly
regret the loss of a good headskin.

The female is an insignificant looking animal, with horns of
about ten or eleven inches in length.   I have never shot one,
so I cannot give any measurements or weights.   A full-grown
buck will scale 240lbs., and sometimes more.

No one should start on a trip after this game unless he is
prepared to exercise the greatest patience, and to show the
most dogged perseverance.   Big bags of fine Ibex are made,
but I have never heard of a big bag of fine Markhor, and should
think myself well repaid by obtaining one fair shot for each

3

fortnight on the shooting ground. The best bags I know of were as follows: A sportsman wintering near Gilgit bagged 13 Markhor, the largest was 48 inches; none of the others coming up to 40 inches in length. Another gun bagged 9 animals in Kashmir, the largest was just under 50 inches, and a few were very fair heads. A third bag was 11 animals with one fairly good one. Shooting Markhor, to make a numerically big bag, must simply be killing a number of animals whose heads the gunner is ashamed to show.

CHAPTER V.

IBEX (*Cupra Sibirica*).

In Kashmir, Keyl ; in Ladak, Skyin ; in Astor, Mayar.

THE dimensions of a full-grown male from the Wardwan were—

Height at shoulder.	Length of body.	Tail.	Weight.
38 inches	... 54 inches	... 8 inches	... 188lbs.

The heaviest weighed was 208lbs.; the head and horns 36lbs.; but this animal was decidedly above the general size. A female stood 32 inches, and scaled 104lbs. The average length of horns of the female is 10 inches. Any horns over 35 inches round the curve are worth preserving; if over 40 inches, they·are fine; 45 inches and upwards are rare.

Since writing my letter to the *Asian*, I have seen some very good horns, and therefore add them to the list I then gave.

The longest horns I have personally inspected are—

Length.	Girth.	Locality from whence obtained.
50 inches	... 11 inches	... Not known.
50 „	... 10 „	... Tilail (Kashmir).
49 „	... 11 „	... Lidarwat (Kashmir).
48 „	... 12 „	... Krishnye (Wardwan).
48 „	... 10 „	... Boonji.
48 „	... 10 „	... Pamir (brought down by traders).
48 „	... 10 „	... Kulsi (Ladak road).
46 „	... 12½ „	... Krishnye.
45 „	... 13 „	... Ditto.

together with a few more of 45 inches in length which mostly came from the Wardwan, but one of which was from the Sindh valley above Gugangair. Doubtless larger have been and still will be shot.

There is a well-authenticated case of a 52-inch head from Gilgit and of 51 inches from Krishnye, and also of a 54-inch from beyond Gilgit. This last requires confirmation, but the two former I quite believe in.

Measurements not made by myself I cannot vouch for; and whenever such are quoted, I shall invariably mention the fact.

Measurements made by shikaris are simply rubbish; they run the tape into the spaces between the knots of the horns, and thus obtain several extra inches.

Ibex are still plentiful. In fact on almost every large range of high altitude in Kashmir, and in parts of Ladak, they still exist. Even on the Manasbal hills a 44-inch head was obtained in December 1877, but I do not think the Lidarwat cliffs will again yield a 49-inch horn.

To make a certainty of seeing large massive horns, a sportsman must now wander far. The best localities are perhaps
the Krishnye, as far up as Nunkun glaciers, with its off-
shoots the Zaisnye, Birbul, and Dichnye and the Kair nullah.
The smaller ravines in the Wardwan are almost shot out.
Soroo is essentially an Ibex country, and has three famous
nullahs, of which the Phoo is the best. The Kaintul ravine,
two marches from Sooknis, is also good ground ; and there long
horns, which are usually slender, are often obtained. In point
of numbers possibly Soroo holds the most prominent position.

Pensela, beyond Ringdum Monastery, is not much shot over,
and would, in all probability, well repay a visit. Opposite
Ringdum is the Kangi. Pensela can be reached from Soroo,
and from the Leh road from Dras. It is marked on the
route map. The ground looks as if it were made to hold game,
but it was quite blank in the summer of last year (1881). I
have already mentioned many places on the Baltistan side, so
will adhere to the line of country on the eastern side. Few
men who are quietly marching along the Leh road know how
close they are to good Ibex ground. The Kulsi and Basgo
nullahs, if shot over with the aid of some one knowing the ground,
should amply repay a visit. By far the finest collection of
male Ibex I ever saw were in a glen not two marches from Leh.
Beyond Leh there is a good place two marches above Runbeer
Bagh, called the Shingshir. (Map, Chap. IX.) It divides into
three small heads, and all these three hold Ibex. Formerly
the Ibex in the vicinity of Leh were driven by large gangs
of Ladakis, and actually forced to come down hill to the guns
of the sportsmen. It seems rather a sacrilege to drive Ibex
that could be stalked, but every one to his own taste. In
the last drive that took place three heads, well over forty
inches each, were secured, and several smaller ones were also
bagged. Beyond, or to the eastward of Shingshir, I know of
no Ibex ground. By marching to Leh by the Zaskar river
some good country would be passed through ; and this march,
taken in conjunction with a visit to Ovis Ammon ground, is
quite within the compass of a six months trip. To mention
every place where Ibex could be bagged would be to fill several
pages ; but I must not omit some of the country above
Bundipoora. In Bundipoora nullah a 42-inch head was bagged
last year. Both the Gugai ravines are good, but the Kheyl
ravine in the Kishengunga direction, although once famous, is
now absolutely denuded of Ibex. In Pangi there are plenty
of Ibex; but, although I have often heard of that part being
the place, I must remain unconvinced ; a really good head is
decidedly the exception. The Sutlej valley Ibex are generally
small ; the only large horn I have seen was on a temple near
Chitkul on the Baspa river. To return to Kashmir. Bhutko-

lan and Goomber, both of which are marked on the map, and can easily be found by looking to the east of Soonamurg, are not bad places to fall back on when most of the good shooting grounds have been secured; but the sportsman should first try to secure Sooknal, which is a few miles beyond, in the direction of Dras. Rewil and Kolan ravines which join the Sindh river below Soonamurg are also a refuge for the late comer. Again the rocks above Kolahoi and towards Amarnath hold Ibex, and doubtless now and again a large head. Commencing, however, with Bhutkolan, all the places I have lately mentioned, except perhaps Sooknal, are only to be looked on as refuges for the destitute. In this class I would enter most of the smaller Wardwan streams, such as Gumber, Kuruz, and Moongil, also the Gweenye. In the autumn months I have known Ibex to be bagged in Bodsar opposite to Gumber; and as it is close to stag ground, it is not a bad place to visit. Up the Sunyan, at the head of the Wardwan, and in the adjacent ravines of Wishni, I never saw a single Ibex, although the country had not been disturbed, and it was not late in the season. (Map Chap. XII.) For the Ibex ground iu Baltistan, &c., see Map of Baltistan in Chapter IV.

The best months for following this sport are April and May. June also is fairly good. Then the Ibex descend in the mornings and evenings to crop the green grass, which shoots forth as soon as the snow is melted. It is heart-breaking work walking up and down the mountain sides in July and August. The whole country is open for the animals to roam over; and nothing but the most wonderful luck will give a good bag at that season.

When once a good head has been seen, do not be in a hurry to give in. Ibex, if not frightened, stop long in the vicinity of the same feeding grounds; and in the end, patience and careful stalking will often prove successful. I know of few descriptions of sport where luck enters less iuto the field than in Ibex-shooting in May. Patience and steady shooting are what are necessary. A man does not require to be a first-rate walker or a really brilliant shot during that season; but he does require to be enduring, and not too eager about getting up at once to bis game.

Year by year the better class of nullahs invariably yield good bags, unless by some misfortune they have been secured by men who simply would never make sportsmen. One thing is to be said—the good shooting grounds are some considerable distance from Srinaggar, and consequently a great deal of trouble has to be gone through before all the arrangements for supplies can be made. In Soroo flour is easily to be obtained, but for the Krishnye every grain of rice has to be drawn from Changus. Men who are not keen on sport will not go so far as the head of the Krish nullah, so that there is every chance, at any rate, of a good account being given of the Ibex met with. (For route see page 7.)

The great drawback to shooting in the vale is the crush and racing against other men for the possession of certain coveted spots. The Krishnye generally falls to the first arrival, and is rarely vacant after April 1st. The second comer either takes the Zaisnye, or else goes as hard as he can travel for some of the Soroo shooting grounds. Gugai is also early secured. There is, however, no reason to despair of making a good Ibex bag, the Ladak nullahs are seldom occupied, and a "travelled" shikari who is worth his salt will, under any circumstances, be able to get his employer a few shots at some fair heads. Many men who arrive in Kashmir a little late, say by May 1st, declare that "all the nullahs are taken up; it is no use going out," consequently they potter about and try in spots where good Ibex have ceased to exist; whereas, if they would only get well clear of the valley, they would find endless vacant ground towards Ladak, either on the direct route over the Zogila, or else by one or other of the roads I have previously mentioned in a former chapter.

Possibly no description of sport gives more latitude to the Kashmir shikari than Ibex-shooting. The new comer probably knows nothing about it, and as there are small Ibex almost everywhere, he is dragged off to the nullah nearest the shikari's house, and his eyes gladdened by the sight of a batch of females, and perhaps a few males with horns of 15 inches in length. It is a very common trick for the shikari to say that he knows of a big Ibex in some nullah, of which the name is but little known. There may or may not be Ibex in this place; but all the good nullahs, or at any rate all that are within 100 miles of Srinaggar, are almost certain to be known by at least half a dozen of the visitors, so that it is as well for a man who is on his first visit to make enquiries. The little known spot is either near the shikaris' home, or near that of a friend's into whose hands he wishes to play. The impertinence of some of the shikaris is really sublime. On one occasion, a man was anxious to make a good bag of Ibex, and had consequently hurried ahead; he fell into the hands of a certain shikari who lives near Manasbal. On the strength of the 44-inch horn which I have mentioned at the beginning of the chapter, the crafty Kashmiri kept his master toiling up and down the rocks above Manasbal and in the Chittingool ravine, when he might have had the pick of almost any shooting ground in the valley. The machinations of the wily but lazy shikari at first appear deep, but their lying is clumsy and easily discovered after a short time; but before the discovery is made, the delay suffered has caused the loss of good ground. Although nearly all the good shikaris are known to me personally, I must decline to give a list of their names for this reason. No Kashmiri works equally well under two different masters; he will do his best with one Englishman, and the next season, with an equally good and liberal master, he will turn lazy and outrageously grasping.

In Baltistan Ibex are killed in the winter by the aid of dogs. Some of the Balti dogs are very useful in finding wounded game, but it is difficult to buy good ones at any price; moreover, the dogs are often very uncertain in temper.

A herd containing females is much harder to approach than one consisting only of bucks. The way in which a female will stand as sentinel on some commanding rock is aggravating beyond description. The sight of the Ibex is very keen; their hearing and powers of scent must be taken into account, so that an approach down wind or from below is out of the question. If I were given my choice I would sooner make my stalk so as to arrive at the same level, as the Ibex then run upwards, and often afford a succession of shots; whereas, if approached from above, they bolt off down hill, and do not turn upwards again until out of shot.

Ibex are very gregarious in their habits. The rutting season is in the late autumn months; and the kids, frequently twins, are born in May and June.

Possibly the following accounts of two or three stalks may be of interest:—The snow had lately fallen, and the ground was scarcely fit for walking over. Tired of inaction the shikari and I made up our minds to start. Giving a couple of blankets and a luncheon-basket to the coolie, we left our camp at Ladhi-hoio in the Krishnye, one May morning. It was a long difficult walk up to the place, where we had formerly seen some fine Ibex. By the afternoon we reached the entrance to a ravine below the Nunkun peak. On the way we picked up a very fine head intact, belonging to an animal which must lately have been killed by an ounce, or by wild dogs. We were tired, and lay down behind some big boulders. Scarcely had we come to a halt, when we spied a herd which were grazing close down to the stream. Between them and ourselves was a broad sheet of pure white snow—evidently no nearer approach could be made.

That night we lay behind rocks and some huge masses of snow that had lately come down from the glaciers above us. At dawn a coolie went back for some more blankets and cooked food. By mid-day the sun had worked wonders on the newly fallen snow, and the herd had grazed its way upwards, and was busily employed in licking the saltpetre from the rocks. By the afternoon we had got into position, and were waiting for the Ibex to descend. Down they came and passed within

300 yards of us. It was tantalizing work, and once I went so far as to take a steady sight at the biggest; but no—it was too far for a certainty. The herd suspected nothing, so we crept back to our hiding place behind the snow; and again spent another night in the open. In the morning, as the Ibex were not visible, and the snow had now melted sufficiently to allow of comparatively safe walking, we ascended the ravine above the salt lick, and viewed the Ibex in a first-rate position for a stalk. The wind was steady, and a short climb brought us to within seventy yards of two fine bucks and a few females, which were lying apart from the main herd. A female whistled its alarm note, but it was too late; the largest male fell, and the others bolted downwards. The left barrel unfortunately knocked over a nanny which was following close behind the second big one. This shot thoroughly scared the others, and they scattered. One or two were foolish enough to linger and gaze around, so taking up the second rifle I had time to fire both barrels, and a second buck rolled over and over stone dead. The tape was soon stretched on the horns, and 46 and 32 inches jotted down in my note book. We turned back and reached Turring-hoie, where the camp met us, and thoroughly enjoyed a good night's rest and not-to-be-despised dinner. This was a satisfactory ending to a rather tedious undertaking, but every stalk is not so fortunate in its results.

One cold wintry morning, very early in April, the snow was falling in Gweenye, when the shikari saw some fiue Ibex not far above the tents. The cliffs above us were quite inaccessible even to a wild goat; and to get a shot a long detour had to be made. The weather did not look promising, but the Kashmiri declared that the day would clear. We started, and climbed for hours; sometimes snow fell, and sometimes the sun shone. Towards mid-day the clouds hung in heavy masses half-way up the mountain, and, oh! it was cold! To add to our discomfort the wind rose; it partially dispersed the clouds, and in the afternoon, when we had arrived at the spot where we thought the Ibex must be, only light thin sheets of vapour were flying about. The glasses were useless in the mist, but we made out a herd, and also made what we considered a good stalk, but no large Ibex were to be seen. There was absolutely nothing that the wildest imagination could fancy to be over 25 inches. Our big bucks had vanished, and worse than all, we were bound to be benighted. Luckily the snow had ceased to fall, and we were able, with a little digging, to clear a space to sleep on; but one blanket, and no fire, which, alas! meant no hot tea, are not much luxury on a cold night.

The morning broke clear and frosty, and the first sight that met our eyes were the big ones again; seven of them, all with horns, certainly over 30 inches, and one amongst them was a beauty. What the length was I cannot say; for the wind changed during the stalk, and away went the herd, never more to be seen by us.

On the way into camp we came on a Ther; we could scarcely believe it, but there was no doubt about it. The stalk again was a failure, the wind was here, there, and everywhere, and the snow began to fall.

Many a successful stalk is made under cover of a passing snowstorm. Once, in the Zaisnye, I got in amongst a herd; the clouds were heavy, and took a long time to lift; the Ibex were uneasy, and twice a female gave its note of alarm, but on the clouds suddenly lifting, there was an old buck standing chest on within fifty yards; several others of the herd were within one hundred paces. Luckily for them most of the heads were not worth having, for without exaggerating, nothing but the most indifferent shooting could have saved four or five of them. After two had fallen, how the shikari begged for the shooting to continue! but it was no use; meat was not required, and that is the only excuse, although a poor one, for slaughtering the small males. The shikari naturally would have liked to have had the whole herd lying dead, for he would then have been able to add considerably to the numbers of the total; and when talking to other employers to relate how he brought to bag so many buck Ibex in the Zaisnye.

Large bags of Ibex can sometimes be got, without condescending to shoot very small ones. A reasonably good shot who perseveres ought certainly to succeed in getting ten fairly good heads if he spends two months in good shooting ground. Amongst his ten or a dozen heads he certainly might expect to have one or two about 40 inches in length, and the remainder to vary from 28 to 35 inches.

The Krishuye last season gave its occupant twelve heads, some of which were large and some were small. The season before it yielded fifteen heads, none of which were under 25 inches; and three were over forty. On both occasions the sportsmen were only a few weeks in the nullah, and on their leaving, it was at once re-occupied by others. Not many years past twenty-two Ibex were killed in this famous nullah by a sportsman, who spent nearly the whole of his six months' leave encamped above Furiabad.

A wounded Ibex or Markhor should seldom be lost, for Ibex especially take to the most difficult places when maimed, and not having their full climbing powers are obliged to pull up before going far. Again Ibex are found in open ground, and even if they cannot be tracked, by watching the neighbourhood, they are almost certain to be brought to bag by the aid of the vultures.

The Ibex are far from tough, and seem to be completely knocked out of time by an express bullet lodged anywhere in the body,

4

CHAPTER VI.

THE THER OR THAR (*Hemitragus jemlaicus*).

In Kashmir, Jagla and sometimes Kras; in Kulu, Kurt.

THE Ther is not very common in any part of Kashmir or in the neighbourhood where I have travelled. It is found in the Pir Panjal, in Kishtwar and Badrawar, and in a few other localities.

Some of the Kashmir shikaris know it by name, and can give tolerably good information as to where it can be met with. Chumba has always been pointed out to me as the place to get Ther, but fortune has never smiled on my endeavours.

An old male, or as it is often called " Jhula," is a difficult animal to stalk; he is generally to be found apart from the herd, and what between his senses of smell and sight, and the prominent position he takes up on some pinnacle of rock, or crest of a hill, he, as a rule, succeeds in getting the best of it. Stalking these very wary bucks is a different business to following a herd. Not many years ago, when engaged in building a new military cantonment, there existed amongst some of us a friendly rivalry as to whom the luck of killing two grand shaggy males would fall. One was never secured, the other I fluked. My old shikari, Gunga, saw the animal standing on a steep precipice, and pointed him out. There was a good deal of mist about, and under cover of some clouds I stalked him. Alas! he fell sheer down some hundreds of feet, and was smashed to pieces. This was hard luck, for I had been after the animal on six or seven occasions.

A few Ther are still to be found not far from the Nag Tiba range near Mussoori, and up the Tonse valley. Again they are fairly plentiful not far from Bôk, and from Chakrata on the road to the Rupin pass.

As a trophy, unless artistically set up, the head does not make much show; but if the long mane, which often reaches to the knees, is carefully dealt with, and plenty of the neck skin left on, it is well worth putting up on a wall.

The largest pair of horns I have seen measured 14 inches, the next were a trifle shorter. Both these specimens were shot in Chumba territory. The horns of the female are very small and insignificant.

During the monsoon the whole herd frequently enters the forests and grazes on the herbage found there, but at other times the Ther frequents the open ground where the grassy slopes are interspersed with gigantic rocks.

In Kashmir and the vicinity, very little attention is paid to the pursuit of this game; but it would be well worth while for any one who has time on hand, after shooting out his Ibex nullah in the Wardwan, to turn down to the country below Maru, for within three marches he will come on very fair shooting ground.

I have seen a Ther in the Gweenye (Wardwan), and my shikari at once called it a Goral! This only shows how easily the names are mixed up, and how confusing it must be for any one who is trying to find out local names. I have also seen a Ther's head which the owner declared was shot in Tilail. I can go no further than to say that my informant evidently thought it had been.

The measurements of a really fine buck Ther, and that of a good Ibex, are almost identical; but the Ibex is the heavier of the two in actual weight, although as Kinloch (1 believe) remarks, the Ther appears to be heavier made.

CHAPTER VII.

THE SEROW (*Nemorhœdus bubalina*).

In Kashmir, Ramoo ; in the Himalayas generally, Serow.

A WRITER in the *Asian* took exception to the name of *Ramoo* being given by Dr. Jerdon as the Kashmiri for the Serow; and, if I mistake not, said that the Goral was thus called. In the locality he was writing about, both animals are rarely to be met with, and his shikari probably confused the names. As previously mentioned, I heard a Ther called a Goral, and I have also had a shikari obstinately apply to the Serow the same term. All the Kashmir shikaris from the western and central portions of the valley have a confused idea of what Ther, Goral, and Barking Deer are. They know that towards the Kishtwar side such animals exist, and that is the limit of their knowledge.

In the winter months Serow can be found with comparative ease in the Sindh valley. For choice of localities I should visit the rocks near Ooraposh, and near the Murg above this place. Also Kutchnumbul, on the other side of the river, and again beyond at Marmar and Koolan.

There is a certain find twelve miles above Ooraposh, at a place called Akabal. (See Map in Chapter XII.)

In the summer try Bur-murg above Akabal, and also at the head of the Phak ravine, and immediately above Shalimar. In the Liddar valley, Serow are to be found near Vesirren, and on the rocks above the deserted village of Kellan.

This game is not often shot by the visitor to Kashmir, and I cannot bring to mind, having seen more than a dozen heads brought in by various sportsmen.

In the outer ranges it is much more plentiful. The valleys of the Tonse and Pabar rivers, the ranges of hills in the Nahun territory, and in the Ganges and Jumna valleys, in fact all precipitous rocks which are interspersed with bushes and trees, afford a retreat for the Serow.

Horns of ten inches in length should satisfy the visitor to Kashmir. Both sexes have horns. The following are the best I have secured, but have seen bigger measurements given by others :—

Sex.	Ht. at shoulder.	Weight.	Length of horn.	Locality where shot.
Male ...	37 inches.	190lbs.	12 inches.	Ganges valley.
Do. ...	38 ,,	190 ,,	10 ,,	Kumaon.
Female...	33 ,,	120 ,,	10 ,,	Budraj near Dehra.

The Serow can often be successfully driven, but the shikari should have a first-rate knowledge of the locality ; for on being disturbed, the animals dash wildly down hill, continuing their course until they have found a secluded spot, where they lie concealed ; or else, after a short stay, work their way, leisurely, to the right or left.

One sportsman, who had spent two months trying to get a pair of horns, ended by killing his game when within two short marches of Srinaggar city. Another man worked hard, but without success ; ho met a friend who was after bears. This friend had a Serow's head, and as he expressed it, he "fluked it by a snap shot." This is the shortest and best description I can give of Serow-shooting. It is very little use to lay one-self out for the sport, but any one who does much shooting in the Himalayas is sure to get a trophy or two.

All the Serow I have shot have either been driven or have been killed by snap shots in the forests, and generally when I least expected. I never had but one chance of stalking a Serow, and that was spoilt by wild dogs suddenly appearing. A wounded Serow will charge a dog, and is not unlikely to bring it to grief. I could never quite make out whether the following was a determined charge at a coolie, but give the story as it occurred :—

I was following a wounded Serow, and a Scotch terrier was running in front. Suddenly the animal I was after dashed out from under a small deodar tree, sent the dog spinning into the snow, then rushed up against a coolie who was slightly in advance, and to whom I was passing up a rifle from below, knocked him clean over, and was past me like a flash. No damage was done, as there was plenty of snow to fall on. The dog picked himself up, and warily took to the track ; but on bringing the Serow to bay, was careful not to expose him-self to any more assaults.

A great number of the so-called charges made by wild animals are only efforts to escape ; but this looked like the real thing, for the Serow was not at all hampered in its move-ments, and could as easily have bolted in the opposite direction. Since this article appeared in the *Asian,* a friend has told me almost a similar story ; only he had no soft snow to come down on.

CHAPTER VIII.

THE GORAL (*Nemorhœdus Goral.*)

In Kashmir, Pijur ; in Ghurwal, Goral.

THE majority of the Kashmir shikaris have never seen a Goral, for this animal is not found in many of the localities to which the visitors generally resort. The Kishtwar country is the best ground, but no one would journey so far to shoot this game.

It happens that I have shot a great many Goral, and have certainly seen hundreds of horns in temples, and brought round for sale, but all my measurements fall short of those given by a well-known sportsman, who mentions nine inches as the average length of horns.

Jerdon's measurements are generally supposed to be average ones, and he puts down "horn 8 inches."

Anyway here are the sizes of the largest specimens I have recorded :—

Ht. at shoulder.	Weight.	Length of horn.	Where shot.
26 inches	....	... 7½ inches	... Ghurwal.
28 ,,	... 59 lbs.	... 7¼ ,,	... Siwaliks.
28 ,,	... 63 ,,	... 8 ,,	... Kumaon.
28 ,,	... 58 ,,	... 8½ ,,	... Bussahir.

Besides these, I have noted a few over seven inches, most of which come from the vicinity of Simla and other hill stations. The longest horns I have seen belonging to a female were five inches.

Goral stalking is very pretty sport, and is excellent practice, both as regards walking and shooting.

They are still to be found close to many of the sanataria, and when no better game is at hand, a pleasant day can be spent in their pursuit. Of course I am not acquainted with a tenth part of the best Goral ground, but here are some localities—

Budraj, near Mussoori ; the open ground between Mussoori and the Rupin pass ; both sides of the road between Deoban and Rama Serai (this country is mentioned in the chapter on Burhel) ; the rocks above the Tonse river ; the sides of the Parbar stream, and the road between Tiri and Nyuee Tal. It is now some years since I turned out into camp for the purpose of Goral-shooting. I give the result of twelve days' shooting solely for the benefit of those who declare that the vicinity of hill stations is utterly shot out.

November 16th, 1876.—Started from Chakrata late in the afternoon, went down the nullah below the dâk bungalow, and turned off to the right towards the Jumna river ; halted about 7 miles out.

November 17th.—On to Lodhona, about 19 miles. The rope bridge over the Jumna river looked quite rotten, so swam over. Shot two kaleege pheasants.

November 18th.—Off at daylight; took the path on the north side of the hill, and reached Josanoo (12 miles). Kaleege and koklas very plentiful; got five brace without leaving the path. The dogs brought them down. A barking deer also bounded across the road.

November 19th.—Missed a barking deer found near the camp. Went on to Bunaree, and wasted all the day after a bear. Saw some khakur, but did not fire.

November 20th.—Again wasted more time after the bear. On the way back to camp shot a brace of koklas and a black partridge.

November 21st.—Marched to More-tâtâ, a pleasant stroll of seven miles. Shot a khakur close to Bunaree; got into camp by mid-day; saw some monaul, but they were wild beyond description. After tiffin went out, saw a Goral standing on a rock; it was stamping with its fore feet, and looking down; made out a leopard crouching under a bush. On getting the bullet the beast growled and disappeared into a cave which was close at hand. Knocked over the Goral as it was bolting away.

November 22nd.—Spent the whole morning trying to get the leopard out, but had to give it up. Smoke, fire, and squibs were of no use. On the way back into camp saw a Goral, and after a long stalk, missed him clean. Afterwards came on another, killed him; both barrels of the express went off, and the hammers cut open my forehead, and gave me a bad headache.

November 23rd.—Marched towards the Jumna. Saw a couple of cock monaul, but they were hopelessly wild. Killed a brace of koklas.

November 24th.—Arrived at the Jumna. Sat up for a leopard which never came.

November 25th.—Fired a snap shot at a Goral, killed it, but found that I had got a very poor pair of horns. Was nearly into camp, which was on the ridge above Kurna village, when some men volunteered to show me bears. Came on the bears suddenly. Again both barrels went off, but as the old she bear was only ten yards off, she got the benefit of the two bullets. Killed a cub with a bullet from the smoothbore. After a long chase bagged the she bear. Had rather a bad fall, the bank gave way, and brought us all down. One of the coolies was damaged and bled a great deal. Got into camp late.

November 26th.—Spent the day attending to the villager. Shot a brace of chikore close to camp.

November 27th.—Chakrata. Got one chikore, two black partridges and five kaleege. The bag was nothing out of the way, and is about what could be expected. More-tâtâ is the same distance from Mussoorie that it is from Chakrata. From there, the pathway leads on to Bôk, and to some fairly good ground for Ther and Serow, but to reach this a month's leave would be required. The shikaris residing in Bunaree know the country well.

The Goral is not gregarious, although several may be found scattered over one hill side. They evince a marked preference for certain spots, and will put up with a great deal of bullying before taking to other localities. They are often to be found within a couple of miles of the villages.

In the rains of 1873 I was living in the Siwaliks. One evening I spied a Goral on a ledge of rock; above the cliff was broken up into small platforms, and below was an unbroken drop into the Ret Rao. Suddenly a leopard rushed out from one of the recesses above the Goral; it missed its aim, but the Goral fell sheer down into the stony bed of the river, and was killed. There are some famous spots for Goral in the Siwalik hills, and if it had not been for the intense heat, I should look back to my long sojourn amongst the Sambhur, the Cheetal and the Goral with great pleasure. As it is, I have nasty visions of being half-stifled in the summer, and dosed with quinine all the rains. Still those ranges are happy hunting grounds, and for any one who wants sport, the crests of the hills, with a camp a short distance below, would prove the places to satisfy him. It is quite useless to do what most people are content to do, that is to pitch on the forest line, and expect the game to visit them. Nothing but confiding doe Cheetal will do this, but high up it is a very different story.

There are some rocks about two miles above the Kasumbri temples which always hold Goral. Above Kalawallah on the right bank of the stream there are some rather arid looking hills, which are a sure find. Again *close* to the big wall on the top of the Timli pass is a good spot to visit.

CHAPTER IX.

THE OVIS AMMON—*In Thibet Nyan.*   OVIS POLII AND KARELINI.

Ovis Ammon.—The difficulty of obtaining specimens of this fine sheep is made the most of by many writers, nor is it as rare, nor as difficult to obtain, as some sportsmen would have us believe.

The Ovis Ammon is possessed of the sense of smell to a remarkable degree, and as everyone who has stalked in Ladak is aware, the wind is treacherous. If the stalker feels a puff of wind on his back, when within seven hundred or eight hundred yards of the game, he well knows it is "all up."

On the tops of the mountains and in the vicinity of glaciers, these puffs of wind are of frequent occurrence; often they will only last for a few seconds, but that is sufficiently long to ruin the chance of getting a shot at the Ovis. Except for this one fact, I cannot admit that the Nyan is harder to approach than any other hill sheep.

Stalking in Ladak is very often a matter of time. Many of us will march for a month to get on to Ovis Ammon ground, and yet will not consent to wait a few days after the game is sighted. Naturally, in a country where the hills are devoid of cover, the game is often seen on spots where it is useless trying to approach it; but if watched for a few hours, it is almost certain to graze its way into a more favorable position. Avoid going after game on gusty and cloudy days, and exercise patience, remembering that you have probably marched some hundreds of miles to obtain a few shots, and one or two days more or less work can make but little difference. I apologise to the experienced stalker for this long lecture. My excuse is, that a good Ovis Ammon's head is often absolutely thrown away for want of a little care.

I will suppose a hardworking sportsman to have reached Leh by May 10th, and to be bent on getting some Oves heads. He has probably arrived a little ahead of others, and besides Ovis Ammon he has a haukering after other game, and wishes to visit the Changchenmo country before it is shot over. Changchenmo is not the best route to take for Ovis Ammon, but I think, if the reader will follow the line of country I mention, he will secure two or three good heads. Tankse village is fifty-five miles from Leh, on the far side of the Changla pass. There the visitor hires carriages. He then moves to Pobraong, doing the distance of thirty miles in three stages; for it is a mistake to press the baggage animals, as at this season they are in wretched condition. From Pobraong, send the camp on to the foot of the Marsemik pass and work round to the right (eastwards).

Early in the year, Ovis Ammon are found close to Pobraong, but later on, after May 15th, they must be sought for high up in the mountains. By Changchenmola and by the Changchenmo stations, No. 1, there is good ground; again across the Marsemik, near Rimdi, and by Rimdi Guinlay on the left bank of the stream, there is an almost certain find. A good plan after reaching Guinlay is to send the camp to Pamzal, and then to cross the stream and work your way over the mountains, keeping to your left front.

You will reach a very large stream, which goes straight to Pamzal. The distance by road is about eight miles; by the hill side possibly twelve or fourteen miles. At Pamzal, you are in the Changchenmo valley, and must not expect to see Ovis Ammon until you have again got on the mountain tops.

My advice is, go to Kyam, eleven miles, then on to Ning rhi, which is about ten miles distant; from there go to Troakpo Kurbo, giving a day or two to the high ground on the right hand side. You are now over the frontier, and will be amused at the wonderful stories the Yak-drivers will invent. There is, however, nothing to fear. The Rudok men never visit this place, for it is a howling wilderness; and if no attempt is made to cross the Kepsang or Demjor passes, there is no chance of meeting any one except a Chauthan shepherd. Between the Troakpo Kurbo ravine and the Demjorla is the best ground. High up under the glaciers, the grass is green early in the year, and this country is not disturbed. In eight days I saw the following flocks:— June 6th, four rams; June 7th, one ram and again ten rams; June 8th and 9th were spent after wounded game; June 10th, blank; June 11th, blank; June 12th, two rams; June 13th, ten rams. Now, assuming that I saw the same animals twice over on some occasions, still I could not have come across less than eighteen or twenty in these eight days. I have omitted any males which I saw with the females, for at this time of year they were sure to be small ones.

The heads of the Silung Burmah and of the Silung Kongma ravines hold very good rams. The best way to reach them is to go up the latter from Kyam, and then cross from there into the Silung Burmah. This ravine has two branches at its head, and both are frequented by this sheep. It is at certain times of the year a difficult place to take a camp to; and if the sportsman objects to sleeping out, he had better leave this beat alone during June; for then the mountain torrents are likely to drench all his baggage, if carried on yaks up the only road by which they can pass. When I have mentioned the Kobrang

Missing Page

ravine (above Gogra), I have exhausted the Changchenmo country.

North of the Indus, the only other Ovis Ammon ground I know of, is by the Mirpa Tso and the Thatoo La. South of the river, there is a large extent of country. Leaving Leh, the traveller can make straight for Marsalang, about twenty-three miles; then to Upchi, eight miles; then to Gya, sixteen miles; and then on to the head of the nullah, which is about five miles.

Here Gya ravine branches into two. Of these two, the right hand one, called the Kayma, is the better ground; the left hand or Tubbuh ravine holds only females. The Kayma nullah is however much shot over, and may or may not hold a good flock. From Gya cross the Tagalang pass and go to Debring and Zara. Here is a first-rate place, called Khanak, the ravine goes towards the Zaskar river. The higher ground is the best.

On through the Rupchu country to the Tso Morari lake towards Hanle, and then up through Lanak and the country described by Kinloch in his work on Himalayan sport. Few sportsmen shoot in Tiri. It is difficult to get at, and in the summer the Indus bars the way; but during the month of May the road is generally open. During the months of June and July there is a road from the Kayma ravine which crosses the head of the shooting ground above Tiri.

There is plenty of ground in the direction of the Niti which holds Ovis Ammon, and sooner than take the trouble to march from Rawal Pindi to the Indus valley shooting ground, or still further to the Rudok territory on the borders of Changchenmo, a distance roughly of five hundred and fifty miles, I should go towards the Niti and Laptel.

Whilst advocating a visit to Changchenmo, early in the year, I do not do this with regard to obtaining general shooting.

Kinloch and others advise the months of July and August.

As far as regards Antelope and Burhel shooting, and a better chance of good weather, I certainly agree. The climate in May is very trying, but it is easier to get over the rivers when frozen over than to wade through them when swollen by the melting snow; and moreover at that season where there is grass, there will the game be found.

There is a great deal of country which is very little visited by Europeans, but about which it is difficult to obtain information. Ladak holds a quantity of game, but not on the beaten track. The Tartar is passively obstinate and obstructive creature, and new shooting ground must be ferretted out by the sportsman, with little or no aid from the inhabitants.

Very few men have been down the Changchenmo river from
Pamzal to the Shyok river, and very few men have tried the
ground between the Changla and Kayla passes. Ovis Ammon
heads are to be picked up in both those places. I confess it
is difficult to get about on unknown tracks : but unless first
on the ground, it is impossible to get a good bag over the well-
known and hackneyed districts.

So much for locality ; now as to size. I have argued that
Ovis Ammon are more plentiful than is generally supposed to
be the case, but large horns are rarely obtained. The largest
I have measured was 45 inches long by 20 inches in girth.
The largest I have shot in Thibet measured 41 inches in length
by 18½ inches in girth. Horns of 38 inches by 17 inches are
fairly common, but the average size killed are from 33 inches
to 34 inches in length, by 16 inches in girth. A very heavy
well-fed ram weighs as much as two hundred and eighty pounds,
the average weight in the spring not being over two hundred
and fifty pounds. From 46 to 48 inches may be said to be the
height of a full-grown male. The female is smaller, and has
much straighter horns, of about 20 to 24 inches in length.
The male can be easily distinguished at long distances by his
white neck and chest. Once I was sorely tempted to shoot a
female. I was short of food for the coolies, and they were on
half rations ; besides, the shot was such a nice one. In fact,
I had argued myself into the idea that it was the right thing
to do. On looking among the loose stones, I saw three lambs
lying besides the mother, and of course the murder was now
out of the question. A female Ovis Ammon that could bring
forth three young into the world, at one birth, deserved to be
spared at any cost. On two occasions I have seen twins, but
never before triplets. In order to see that there was no mistake, I waited until the mother moved off. She was accompanied
by all three young ones, and there was no other Ovis in sight.

As it turned out, the coolies did not suffer, for I got two
rams the next morning.

Closely allied to the Ovis Ammon is a sheep styled by
naturalists Ovis blanfordi. Besides these, the gigantic Ovis
polii and Ovis karelini are found in Central Asia. As I
before stated in Chapter III, these live beyond the range of
sportsmen. Since writing this Chapter, I have heard that
Government have forbidden Europeans to visit Yarkand ; consequently, any hope of reaching the hunting grounds where
these grand trophies might be obtained, is for the present at an
end. To attempt to reach the resort of Ovis polii by the Gilgit
route would be sheer madness. The fanatical tribes inhabiting
the borders of the Maharajah's dominions would soon put a
stop to the enterprise.

A Scotch merchant who came down from Yarkand in the summer of 1882 brought down six pairs of horns. They were picked up in the Pamir, and brought down for sale. The prices realized were high; as much as five hundred rupees was bid for the best pair. The largest pair of horns were 61 and 62 inches measured round the curve. The smallest pair were 54 inches: even these were sold in Leh for Rs. 125.

The merchant had, however, to send out fifteen marches from Yarkand in order to get the horns picked up, and carriage from Yarkand has lately become very expensive. Larger horns have been obtained, and a photograph of a pair, which were measured as 73 inches round the curve, has been procurable in Debra for some months past. This pair of horns was brought down to the resident of Gilgit in 1881. I confess to getting very puzzled over the difference between Polii and Karelini. At one time I thought I knew them apart, but now that I have seen a good many heads, am fairly puzzled. I therefore fall back on my preface, and leave the subject to naturalists.

The Map attached to this Chapter shows several places which are mentioned in Chapters X, XI, XV and XVII.

CHAPTER X.

OVIS VIGNEI (*Sharpoo of Ladak ; Oorin of Boonjie and Astor*).
THE OORIAL (*Ovis cycloceros*).

I REGRET to state that I have lately lost my measurements of
this animal ; but can quote from my general notes the sizes of
several very large pairs of horns. In the possession of a
gentleman, a resident at Leh, I saw a pair of horns 36¼
inches in length, and 11¾ inches in girth. This certainly
seems huge, but still is perfectly accurate. The horns are now
in Simla.

At Snurla, Ladak, there is a pair of horns lying on a pile of
heads ; they measure 32 inches in length ; and close to Leh are
horns of 33 and 34 inches. An average horn is about 26 inches,
and a good one anything over 29 inches.

From Boonjie I have seen nothing over 28 inches, but attribute this to chance.

In Ladak I would recommend the following localities :—

Chillingtung above Alchi ; the road lies opposite to Snemo,
and the Indus should be crossed at the bridge by Lardo (See
Index map) ; the lower portions of the Shingshir nullah ; the
ravines above Chimray ; and early in the season above Lama-
Yuru.

Shingshir is not marked on the route map ; it is immediately
above Runbeer Bagh (Tikzay), and is three marches from Leh.

This nullah branches into three ravines, and holds Ibex
above the junction of these tributaries.

In Baltistan in the month of May, or better still in April,
try the Boonjie plain. Later in the year " the Oorin" leave this
plain, and work up both banks of the Astor river, showing
however a greater preference for the left bank. In their migra-
tions they come southwards as far as the Mir Mullick nullah.
(Chapter IV, Map of Baltistan).

Late in the season, when they are widely scattered over the
whole country, they are said to be difficult to find ; but early in
the year they are to be met with in great numbers near the
junction of the Astor and Indus rivers. There is plenty of
other ground that holds Oorin, but none I can bring to mind
that is likely to afford a better chance of procuring a few heads
than the localities described. The winter is *the time* for shooting
this game. The native shikaris lie hid behind walls and in pits ;
and judging by the number of horns they bring for sale, must
succeed in killing a good number of Sharpoo.

Whether it is sheer bad luck or a fact I cannot say, but there appear to be very few big rams. The only large horn I have obtained was from Wanla; it measured 31 inches by $10\frac{1}{2}$ inches in girth. However I once lost a really good one and give the story:—

It was after a long and tolerably hard day's work, whilst I was returning to Camp, that I came on a flock of fifteen male Sharpoo. Amongst them was one beauty, by far the finest head I have ever had a chance of securing. The flock was grazing its way down towards the more level ground, and passed within five hundred yards of where I was standing. As soon as they were over the ridge of the spur, I ran forward and spied them grazing at the bottom of the ravine. They were badly placed for a stalk, and as it was very cloudy, I feared a change in the wind. Accordingly I moved higher up the hill. In about half an hour, the rain fell in torrents, and was succeeded by a cold wind, so I had to return to camp. Once or twice I caught myself cogitating over where I should get the big head set up, and I confess to feeling sure that the bag was to be increased by a very important item.

I fully made up my mind not to spare time or toil, and only to shoot when it was good long odds against the animal. The next morning I found the tracks, and shortly after came on the flock. I left the coolie behind, and crept on alone, but the man managed to show himself, or at any rate to excite the suspicions of the rams, for they stood gazing intently in his direction, and as the top of the coolie's head was visible to me, it very likely was also seen by the Sharpoo. They quietly walked off, and went over a hill. Such a climb as they gave me before I sighted them again! They were grouped together at the bottom of the ravine far below. This time I took the coolie with me, and he behaved with great discretion; but unfortunately a shepherd came up the ravine, and over the next hill went the flock of Sharpoo.

This was getting monotonous, but I wanted that big pair of horns, so went up the hill again, and down on the other side. There they were, stretched on their sides, lying on a sloping hill side. Above them were some cliffs of very irregular formation, and if they would only give me time, I could get opposite to them and fire across the nullah. Time in abundance they gave, and I was within 150 yards, and behind a big boulder hours before the big one would rise. The clouds were bringing up snow or rain, and I was greatly afraid of having to take a running shot if the wind changed.

At last the big one got up, and remained motionless. Crack went the rifle, and the ram dashed downwards, throwing his legs wildly about, and fell with a splash into the stream below.

Why I had not killed him dead I know not. I was a little disconcerted, but fired the left barrel at a second Sharpoo, which was idiotically poking his nose over a rock and staring at me. Bother that second beast, I attribute losing the big one to him. I could not see into the bed of the ravine, and it took half an hour to get round. There were large splashes of blood but no Sharpoo. Rapidly taking up the track of the big one, I sent the coolie to look for the other, but after a short time he joined me. The two tracks had met; a little higher up they again separated, but which was the big one's and which was that of the one hit by the second shot, not even Cooper's Red Indians could have told. The blood was on hard rock, and there was about the same quantity on each track. The snow began to fall, and the traces were quickly getting obliterated. At last up jumped the smaller Sharpoo; he had concealed himself behind a rock, and only got up when I was on him.

Back I ran, for the snow was falling thick, and the blood marks were almost covered, but it was no use; the track turned downwards over ground which was bad going at the best of times, and with snow and sometimes hail driving into my eyes I was quite beaten. I got back into camp long after dark, very, very disconsolate, and in a frame of mind that a really good dinner could not render brighter.

Snow fell for two days, and after it ceased a blazing hot sun soon melted it, but the tracks were gone; all were washed away, except some large splashes of blood where the wounded ram had fallen over the cliffs.

In spite of what has been said about "the biggest being always the lost one," I shall always maintain that he was one of the largest horned Sharpoo in the Himalayas. It will be many a long day before I forget the stalk; and, although since that day I have had great luck after other animals, still I do wish it had held to me on this occasion.

The last Sharpoo I killed was simply idiotic in its behaviour. Evidently he suspected something, but could not make out what was the cause of his being alarmed. The animal came within fifteen paces of me. It was a pretty sight to see him cautiously advance to where I was lying concealed behind two boulders, then suddenly to wheel round and bolt, but it was too late for his safety.

As a rule Sharpoo are very cute, and are nearly, if not quite as quick at getting your scent as is an Ovis Ammon. They can travel over the most difficult and rocky ground, and when hit take to the cliffs, and hide themselves on some ledge on the rocks; consequently they are not easily recovered when wounded.

The young are born in May or June. The horns of the female are short and insignificant. A flock of females is often met with close to the Leh road near Snemo (Index Map), and very often has its ranks thinned by the passing traveller, who cannot resist a shot, after having tramped for days, along a dusty and stony road without once taking his rifle from its case.

The Oorial or Houriar, the wild sheep of the Punjab, occurs on the trans-Indus ranges and in the Hazara hills (Jerdon, page 295). On the salt ranges where it is generally shot by the European sportsman, it is still fairly plentiful. Horns of upwards of 30 inches in length are now and again to be obtained; but far the majority of those brought to bag do not exceed 25 to 26 inches. The chances are against any one obtaining a pair of horns exceeding that length during a fortnight's trip.

A very good bag was made in November 1880, and for any one who has time to spare, and is not tied down to the date of October 15th, it is well worth his while to go for a short expedition, and try his luck among the Oorial or Ovis cycloceros.

The best ground for large heads is near Dil-Jubbah : this is south of Sahowa railway station.

Twenty-five miles from Jhelum, at the back of Tillah on the edge of the range, is Pindsevecca ; seven miles off is Kotul Kund. Both these places may afford sport. The shikari's name is Akbar Alli.

CHAPTER XI.

THE BURHEL (*Ovis Nahura*).
The Narpoo of Ladak.

WHERE to obtain good sized Burhel horns is a question that has taken me long to solve. Iu Ladak there are very few fine pairs to be obtained, but as regards the animals they are more plentiful than any other kind of game. They are not, however, nearly so tame and easy of approach as they were some few years ago. I picked up a couple of good thick pairs of horns, each 27 inches in length, one in the Changchenmo valley, and the other at Chilling on the Zaskar, but I have seen very few of over 24 inches that have been shot in Ladak.

For fine trophies I should recommend going from Mussoori or Simla over the Rupin or Borenda passes. A very pleasant trip could be made by leaving Mussoori on April 15th, reaching Chakrata on the 16th. From there *viâ* Deoban hill to Rama Serai and Jacko, spending a week or so over this portion. Then over the Rupin pass to Sangla and Sangli and up the Buspa river to Chitkul ghat, reaching Chitkul by May 15th. Then over the Nila pass (see small scale route map) into the Bhagiruti valley; or, if preferred, instead of going up to Chitkul work towards Riepa, and back either by Simla or any other chosen road. Three months would amply suffice for visiting any portion of this country, including the nullahs leading down to the Spitti river. Burhel, Ther, Gooral and Serow might be met with. Ibex are found on the far side of the Babeh pass, and from Dankar a road goes to Leh (See Route Map). Khakur also are in places plentiful, and the route lies through scenery which much vaunted Kashmir certainly cannot excel and but seldom equal. Whilst dwelling on this part of the country I may as well mention that in the autumn months the first six or seven marches are good pheasant ground, and near the Tonse river, which could be visited on the way back, there are some fine Sambhur heads to be obtained. Formerly it was not difficult to secure two or three, but now-a-days the big ones seem to have been nearly all killed off. This was done during a very severe winter, but the chances are that these shooting grounds, as they lie adjacent to big reserved forests, will recover themselves.

To return from this digression. Most men who go to Ladak expect to shoot a Burhel, but possibly very few men would care to make this game their primary object, so I will do my best to aid them towards getting a few shots whilst *en route* to the resorts of Antelope or Ovis Ammon.

Of course it is a great object not to lose time when marching for some coveted shooting ground. Accordingly I first mention places that are absolutely on the beaten tracks.

I will suppose the camp is at Tankse, and on the way to Changchenmo. Instead of marching to Muglib let the tents be pitched five miles farther on. The Map gives Tsearh Tso as the name of the place, but it is generally called Chukha Talao. In the months of May and June Burhel are to be found to the right of the main ravine, and in the nullahs which lie to the south of the camping ground. During the spring and summer the ravine, and in fact the whole of the ground above Lukung, holds large flocks of Burhel. Thus, when the camp moves from Tsearh Tso to Lukung, which is about ten miles, or to Pobraong, five miles farther on, the best plan is to turn up the deep gully on the left, and work up this to the flats above. This place is a certain find. I once saw five flocks, aggregating in all one hundred and twenty-nine animals, and on another occasion a fine flock of seventy at the head of this ravine.

From there, by Montol to Pobraong, is a fairly easy afternoon's walk, but late in the year it would be better to drop straight down to Lukung, for if the Koh-loma torrent is in flood, it is difficult to get across. Above Pamzal, Burhel are to be found on the same ground as the Ovis Ammon. Both the nullahs above Gogra hold this sheep, the Kobrang is the better, but the ravine above the hot springs, as far as the Lingzintung plains, has in it a few flocks.

In the Silung Kongma ravine they are also to be found. Then by Shooshal there are a few big rams. Nearly all these places are on known shooting routes, and are easily found.

Off the main routes, there are some very nice ravines near Gya and Miru. The nullahs joining the Zaskar are the best that I know of as far as regard numbers: the easiest route from the Leh side to these shooting grounds is to cross the Indus at Lardo, and then either to make by Alchi and the Strakspir pass into the Sumdab-foo, or else by the Lardo nullah over the Spangling mountain, and drop down on Drogulika; but this latter, although a good shooting route, is very bad walking. There is a road up the Zaskar, which is sometimes open, but it depends on the amount of water in the river (See Index Map).

If the object in view is to shoot Burhel, go by Drogulika; if Sharpoo, work by Alchi. From Drogulika to Hinjo is ten miles, and is an easy march over the Pass. There are three intermediate nullahs between these two places, in one of which I once saw no less than thirteen pairs of horns lying within a radius of half a mile! These horns were nearly all good ones,

and it looked as if the animals had died in some very severe
year. From Hinjo to Lama-Yuru is one long march. Here
you rejoin the road. The Hinjo pass is open by May 15th,
but the Spangling not before June 15th. The Strakspir about
the same time.

Near Wanla, which is the largest village between Lama-Yuru
and Lardo, reside two or three shikaris; it is as well to send
for them and use them as guides. This place, Wanla, is worth
visiting. In the spring there are plenty of Ibex about, but in
the summer they decamp to Fatoksir where it is useless to follow them. Possibly the shikaris may be able to show some
Burhel in May or June, but there appear to be no big rams to be
seen.

It may be taken generally that the ravines joining the left
bank of the Indus, between Lardo and Tiri, hold Burhel and
Sharpoo; those which join the right bank are good for Ibex.

We need scarcely mention other places, except to say that
wherever horns are seen there must be living animals about.
In the vicinity of the Pangong lake the horns are used for
making hoes, and are not put into heaps, hence at Tankse, Lukung,
Chaggra, Man, &c., they are conspicuous by their absence.
For any one visiting Ladak by the Lachalang route, there are
some good spots to be found in Lahoul, but scarcely on the
direct line of march.

Burhel meat is far better eating than the wretchedly bad
mutton which is procurable in Middle Thibet. The favorite
plan of the villagers is to sell to the unfortunate traveller the
old and worn-out weight-carriers' sheep which for years have
toiled about the hills, laden with salt, borax or sulphur. No
human being could possibly eat them, and no beast but a wild
dog could appreciate them. The smaller sheep are the best,
and at any rate are eatable, but it takes really good mutton to
surpass a saddle of Burhel in the months of August and
September.

These animals are utterly impervious to cold, and seem to
prefer the highest mountains. Even in places where the grass
is scanty, and where a piercing cold wind is blowing, the
Burhel, unlike most Thibetan game, does not graze much during
the day time. Sharpoo, on the contrary, are perpetually rising
and feeding, and then lying down again.

Waiting for a Burhel to get up is a tedious affair, but he is a
tough beast to kill, and a shot badly placed is useless. A
broken leg will seldom prove sufficient to allow of his being
brought to bag; he will travel over ground which will test a good
cragsman, and the chances are, that the Tartars will refuse to
follow, for they are not good on rocks or ice. Many a wounded
ram have I lost, and when toiling after them have longed for
a pair of Baltistan dogs to bring them to bay. English dogs

are of no use, for they cannot stand the rarefied air of the great altitudes; moreover they break their toes on the rocks, and not seldom come to grief down some precipice.

A pair of good dogs are valuable beyond price. Here is a story of what once occurred: In Gogra two Burhel had been wounded—one was followed by the sportsman, the other was pursued by two Baltistan dogs. The dogs speedily brought their quarry to bay, and kept it there until the other was disposed of. The ram on the approach of the men ran a tilt at one dog, and sent him flying down the precipice. The other dog turned the Burhel back, and when rejoined by the second, regularly boxed the game up under a rock. Unfortunately the shikari had forgotten the spare cartridge pouch, and the only charge left in the rifle failed to kill. It was too dark to go to camp for more, and the dogs lay out all night, and in the morning were still on the spot watching the ram! This happened in July 1881.

To exemplify the great uncertainty of all shooting I cannot refrain from describing a week spent after Burhel.

July 9th.—Reached the ground where I felt certain of finding any number of rams; not one could be seen. No one had shot the nullah for three years, still it was quite empty. There were no marks of leopards or wild dogs to account for this, and as the 10th and 11th also proved blanks, I made up my mind to leave. The 12th and 13th were snowy, and I could not march. It was only out of desperation that on the 14th I went on to the hill side. It was still snowing; there was a favorite spot above the tents, where, after a very stiff climb, I sat down. Muffled in a blanket I peered into the clouds. The heavy vapour lifted for a few minutes and disclosed two Burhel within five hundred yards. The wind was steady, and before long I had killed one and missed the other. The 15th was fine and clear. From the tents I saw nine rams. Out of these I killed one and wounded but lost another. Then again on the following day I succeeded in getting a good ram, and viewed some more in the evening. Now where had the game come from? Not from greater altitudes, for I was stalking at 17,000 feet elevation, and there were not any higher mountains in the vicinity.

Burhel vary much in size and weight. Of the full grown rams I have weighed the heaviest scaled 150lbs., and the lightest 119lbs. The first was from the Rupin, and the second from the Zaskar country. Possibly a good average would be:—

Ht. at shoulder.	Length.	Weight.	L. of horns.	Girth at base.
33 inches.	52 inches.	130lbs.	22 inches.	11 inches.

In the glare of a Ladak summer's day, absurd as it must seem, I have found it hard to tell the sexes apart, although the

horns of the female are thin and short. The haze on the
stony hills is on occasions very deceiving, and must be seen
to be understood, but the black chest of a ram is a certain
point to discriminate by, and the shikari will nearly always
tell the sex by this at very long distances.

———

CHAPTER XII.

The Stag (*Cervus wallichii*).

The Hangul or Barasingh of Kashmir.

Of late years this stag has gradually been making its way towards the south-east, and has become more numerous in the direction of Kishtwar, Badrawar and Chumba (Index Map). It has been ousted from some of its former summer retreats in Kashmir by numberless cowherds. All game seem to be impatient of the inroads made by tame buffaloes. Old shikaries declare that the wild animals cannot stand the smell of the buffalo. This is very probable, and certainly where the buffaloes pasture, the deer leave. Cows and sheep do not penetrate into the dense recesses of the jungle in the same way as the buffaloes do, and consequently they do not do so much damage. The stag, when he has cast his horns at the end of March or beginning of April, makes his way to the birch forest at the heads of the main glens ; or else crosses the lower passes and enters into the more remote forests on the Kashmir side of the snowy ranges. The game that retires to the far distant forests is not much disturbed, and can pass the period, during which the horns are in course of formation, in comparatively safe retirement.

It is after the renewal of their antlers that the stags make their way back to the lower hills and court the companionship of the hinds, which, as a rule, have remained on the ridges bordering the main valleys of Kashmir proper. It is during this season that the European sportsman has mostly to do with stag-shooting. When, as the Highlanders say, "the stags are roaring," or as it is denominated in Kashmir, "calling," it is the easiest time to kill the Barasingh. There is something about this kind of sport which rather gives one the feeling of being a poacher, for it appears to be taking a mean advantage; but it is the only season when most of the visitors to the valley can get an occasional shot at the stags.

It is now a recognized thing that it is quite correct to take this advantage. I, therefore, will do my best to help the sportsman *to poach* ; for this stag, unlike our own red deer, rarely gives the opportunity for a good open stalk. A good local shikari is an *absolute necessity*, unless one has been over the same ground during a previous year. Every small pool of water, and every stream must be known. Every likely copse where the animals will lie during the heat of the day ; every ridge where they will in all probability call during the evening, the hunter should be intimately acquainted with. More than this, the paths over the mountains, along which the stags make their way to the lower hills, should be visited, and to wander about and find these would be an endless undertaking. Lastly, a local man or two is necessary in order to get information from the villagers as to where a stag calls during the day time. If there is no "native go-between" to sift the men's evidence, you are likely to be told endless lies, and if you get angry and abuse your informant, and refuse "buksheesh," the villagers remain silent for the rest of your stay. All these arguments point strongly to the employment of the Kashmir shikari.

Writing of Kashmir sport, some twenty years gone bye, Mr. Brinkman advocates killing off a few hinds before the calling season. There may then have been something to be said for this destruction, but now-a-days a trigger should never be pulled at a female.

The following was a bag made by a very triumphant shikari not many winters ago—forty hinds and two stags!! The sepoys from the Hurri-Parbat fort come into the Laar district during the winter, and shoot down big and small. It is a thousand pities; but what can be done? Absolutely nothing, except through the Maharajah, and he could very easily put a stop to it. Liberty loving America has in many of its States game laws, but the Autocratic Government of India refuses to protect any animals, but elephants. There are reasons on both sides, and "nil desperandum" is the motto that should be taken up by the promoters of a "close season"—a "heavy gun tax," or better still "game laws." It is almost impossible to get over the fact that the game laws could be used as an instrument of oppression in India; if so what would it not be in Kashmir? As a visitor to the Kashmir dominions, and as one who has been well treated in that country, I wish to avoid all political discussion in these chapters, and so must leave unwritten many things that I should like to put down on paper; for by wintering in Kashmir one sees and hears more than the summer visitor can do.

I remember on one occasion saying that I was inclined to class the stag and markhor horns as *the* trophies to be obtained in the Himalayas. I was met by the remark, no one but a "griff" would care so much for the stags' heads. Well, I am content to remain a "griff," and to adhere to my great admiration of the antlered stag. Later on, it will be seen how little I was able to do during a winter spent in Kashmir, and I confess to a great deal of disappointment over the result. Leave is dear to the Indian sportsman, and leave is alas! limited, so that I doubt if I shall again try the experiment of a whole winter in Kashmir, but some time, perhaps not far distant, I shall do my best to reside in the valley duriug January, February and March.

I must now commence to aid those who wish to obtain trophies during the calling season. One year, the first stag I heard called on the 10th September. I had just before fired at a red bear in a field. After this I did not hear a single call until nearly the end of the month. Another year I heard three separate stags call on the night of 14th September, and again on the 15th; then one on the 16th. After that came rain and the woods were silent for some days. The Regimental Officers have mostly to be back at their stations by October 15th, and cannot, therefore, expect to do much in the calling season, but by leaving Srinaggar for good on September 15th, and taking some nullah in the Sindh or Bundipoora direction, if leaving by Murree, or towards Dandwar if they wish to go out by the Pir Panjal route, they ought to get a few shots. During the commencement of the calling, the bellowing is only heard at night, and the date when they commence to call is, to a great extent, dependent on the state of the weather. The greater the heat the earlier the calling; the finer the weather the more frequently will the stags be heard.

With the exception of the advice to kill the hinds, Mr. Brinkman's chapter on this description of sport is excellent. I only wish that now-a-days I could hold out any hopes of as large a bag as he obtained. A couple of good heads should satisfy any one, or at least should stop any grumbling; but it is quite possible to obtain six or seven pairs of antlers during the season, the dates of which I should put from September 20th to October 15th, or at latest October 20th.

In my letter to the *Asian* I did not enter on localities, but will now do so. The country I know best is in the Liddar and Sindh valleys, and in a lesser degree the vicinity of Nowboog. I have never been out after stags in the Lolab or above Bundipoora, but can guarantee the information given about those parts as being correct. The sources from which I have obtained it are undeniably good.

I will commence on the western side and work along the valley. Due north of Alsoa, which is marked on the map and is on the Woolar lake, is the Lashkot hill, the Kralpoora nullahs, the local name of the more northern branch of which is the "Bow." Then there is the Bundipoora stream, also the Erin. These spots are suitable for October shooting. Very early in the season, say during the commencement of September, try northwards in Gugai and Foolmai. The stags summer in this district, and work down from there to the first mentioned ravines, and also find their way into the Lolab.

Machil, due north of the Lolab, has frequently been pointed out to me as likely to give good sport.

Next comes the Sindh valley; for choice I should secure
Wangat; then I should take Hien or Akahallan, or else should
go to Marmar or Gond. Chittingool is a small but fairly good
place. The drawback to Hien is the dense forest, but the
stags must come through that way; and above the ridge there
is some good country towards Boorzwas, and on to Nagbaran;
but though adjacent this does not belong to the Hien nullah
ground. In the Liddar valley there *are* stags, and some big
ones, but the Gooja's (or cowherd's) huts are numberless.
Aroo and Moondlan, above which are some big murgs, are
likely spots in September. Mainpal above Palgaum is the best
place in the northern part of the Liddar. Above Praslang
there is always a stag or two. Southwards there is a very good
chance of a few shots at Vesirren, and another place is the
Lung-nye. To shoot this, the best place to pitch the tents is
at Lidroo.

On emergency try above Eshmarkam. I must not omit to
mention the Nowboog. It is not a bad district if driving is going
to be resorted to, but my knowledge of the higher portions is
limited to two hurried visits of a few days duration. There is
room for two or three guns. Of the country south of Nowboog
I shall have more to say when dealing with the winter shooting.
If the sportsman has time on hand, Kishtwar direction is now
justly becoming popular; and on the slopes of the Hoksar
there is some very good ground.

I think I have now pointed out sufficient places to ensure
any one getting a vacant nullah or hill side during even a
crowded season. I believe in the lower ground, that is eleva-
tions about 8,000 to 9,000 feet, some men fancy the high ground
amongst the birch forest. It is certainly pleasanter as
far as regards climate; but the stags are only travelling in
the higher altitudes, whereas lower down they seem to settle
into certain spots, and to stop there for days together.

It is very aggravating work when the stags do not call
until just before sunset. Often and often this occurs; not a
sound is to be heard in the day time, but when darkness is
setting in, they begin. On a bright moonlight night it is quite
possible to crawl up to the game, but it is not easy to hit by
moonlight unless within twenty yards, and the grass is
generally too dry to allow a noiseless approach within that
distance. If a stag is seen to be ascending along a ridge
and can be waited for by lying under the slope, thus securing
a view of him against the sky line, there should not be much
difficulty in hitting him. There are, however, so many "ifs"
which come into play during night-shooting that I cannot
really recommend any one to try except over water which is
much frequented by stags. Such spots are Haree above
Marmar, and Burnowboog in Wangut.

Missing Page

The great charm about this shooting is the glorious weather that in all probability continues throughout the calling season. Under any fir tree a pleasant bivouac can be made ; and no tent is necessary on the hill side, although it is a good thing to have a comfortable camp pitched in the vicinity, to which, at intervals, the sportsman can retire for rest and change.

At the end of August, or during the first week of September, many places can be found where the stags come out on to the ridges of the mountains, and rub their horns against the trees, toss about the fern and long grass, and root up the ground with their feet. Occasionally a head or two can be obtained at these spots early in the season, but it is not worth while trying if the hunter is not pressed for time. The horns thus obtained are often slightly covered with velvet ; and sometimes the tips are not quite hard set.

The noise a stag *can* make when "roaring" is much louder than would be imagined, and can be heard at a great distance; but very often, when the animal is lying down, he only utters a prolonged moaning sound. This latter is very deceptive, and unless frequently repeated, it is difficult to find out the exact direction to follow.

I have known the natives copy the louder call so well that a stag has answered the challenge, and deliberately walked out of the forest into the open. Last year a Sindh valley man brought a stag close to our bivouac by imitating the call. It was pitch dark, but it was very amusing to hear the stag coming nearer and nearer ; at last he got our wind, and with a couple of short snorts was off. I was leaving the vicinity the next day, or certainly should not have played these pranks.

It is not half such good fun shooting stags in the dense fir forests as it is in the more open ground ; but if the sportsman finds all the more open country occupied by other guns he should by no means think that he cannot make a good bag. The best collection of horns that I have seen were shot in the forests; of course it is a bore not to know what sized antlers one is after, and not to view the stag until the rifle is being raised for the shot, but it is by no means certain that fir forests, with of course not too much undergrowth, are not the best ground.

I now come to the winter shooting. I am a little uncertain what to say about it. First catch your winter, then be able to get about. There is, I fancy, little doubt that by building one or two rough shelters before the snow falls that the latter difficulty would be got over. The Kashmir authorities would not allow any one to build a hut, but sufficient shelter could be run up with matting, and under that the tents could be pitched. This is incompatible with choosing your winter ; if it could be done, the plan would be not to decide to enter the valley until information of a really heavy fall in December or early in January had been obtained. The late falls of snow do not drive the deer down. The hazel buds are swelling and they can graze on them; the sap is rising in various bushes and trees, and the deer can eat the smaller twigs, but an early fall forces the animals into the valleys. My own experience of a winter's shooting is as follows :—

December.—Got within shot of an eight-tined stag. Saw quantities of females and young ones, but not a single big stag.

January.—No snow, so did not go out.

February.—Very little snow; and then only light falls which melted. Saw one or two small stags, but nothing large until the end of the month. During the last few days of February and early in March there were heavy falls of snow; and before the stags left for their summer quarters, I got within shot of the following :—On one occasion two stags. Shortly after came on five, then again on three, and lastly on a single one. Independently of these, I saw one or two not bad heads, but in positions where it was hopeless to pursue them.

If a man could stand the fleas and other crawling insects found in the villagers' houses, he could easily get about during a severe winter, but the mere thought of it is enough to make most people uncomfortable; not all the heads in Kashmir would induce me to try it.

Walking in the deep snow is weary work, and the nights are very long. It is dark about 4 P M., and it is almost impossible to rouse the servants before 8 A M. A stove is a necessity, but a small tent soon becomes unbearably hot; the door has to be opened, and if the night is windy, it is decidedly unpleasant.

I cannot resist giving my experience after some individual stags, and will, therefore, copy a description of a stalk or two which formerly was printed in the *Asian* :—

I was looking for a woodcock, but had with me a coolie carrying a rifle and a few cartridges. I was not in the least expecting to come on any deer, but I had been bothered by my Rajpoot followers to shoot them a pig. The weather was very cloudy, but it also was windy, so that not unfrequently there were short spells of clearness, and the hill sides could be at intervals seen. During one of these spaces of time I viewed three stags far up amongst the snow. Sending home a coolie with the shot gun, and taking but one man and a spaniel which would not go back, I started for the climb. I was foolish enough to let the man over-persuade me, and it served me right. The wind changed, as it always does towards evening, and although I had arrived near the stags, I had to retrace my steps and begin afresh. Through the snow I and the gun-bearer waded, sometimes up to our knees, and now and again up to our belts. At last the climax came; it began to snow ; still we both struggled on in a stubborn way. This was the second mistake; it would have been far better to have gone back and tried our luck the next morning. To cut short the story I was quite exhausted when I arrived within what I imagined was about three hundred yards of the game. The three had been joined by two others. One stag was a splendid twelve pointer. It was impossible to get any nearer, for the intervening nullah was covered with quite six feet of soft snow ; and besides the stags would have seen us. I tried to fire from the shoulder, but was too much out of breath, so drove the alpeustock into the snow, and used it as a rest. Both the bullets fell short, but three stags still stood. The light was very bad, and the fine snow was driving into my eyes. However the third shot found a billet, and the largest stag plunged forward on to its head. A fourth shot, the shikari declared, hit another, but I do not think it did. Home we had to go, for it was getting dark, and to cover the three hundred yards in that soft snow and on the steep incline would have taken most of the remaining daylight, and the ground on the way back was rocky and steep. I felt nearly certain of finding the stag the next day, in fact expected to get him within a few yards of where he fell. What a journey we had homewards ; the dog's leather leading string I tied on to my waist and pulled the poor little half-frozen beast along until I arrived on firm ground. We were all soaking wet, and soon became very disgusted, for the fine falling snow changed into broad flakes ; and it was unlikely that the wounded game would be found.

All night it snowed hard, and next morning it was heavier work than ever. On carefully removing the snow, we found large patches discolored with the blood, and there was just sufficient of the track left to find out that the wounded stag had separated from the others, and had lain down under some overhanging rocks. Here again was plenty of blood ; beyond this we could not advance. A villager tried and sank up to his shoulders in a fresh snow drift ; then we all tried, but it was useless. I fancy the stag was a dead one, and possibly a visitor to Kashmir will pay the lucky finder Rs. 20 or more, for big antlers fetch high prices. More shame to the buyers, for if the horns were not saleable the shikaris would not be so keen on the winter shooting.

The next day was tolerably fine ; the idea struck me that the stags might have taken to a sheltered spot not more than a mile from where I had lost the big one. This turned out to be the case, for after a good long climb through snow, in

which we often sank up to our waists, whenever we came on a
softish place we found some stags. The only question was
whether the clouds would not cover the mountains before we
could get up to the game. It was no use pottering about and
waiting, but the thing to do was to get it over as sharp as
possible, for the clouds in dense opaque masses were rolling
up the hill sides. I left the Kashmiri behind, and hurrying
along had got within shooting distance, when close to me out
dashed another stag. He was so close that I could not imagine
a miss, but he did not falter. Almost immediately after
firing the shot the clouds were on me. I just made out the
dim outline of a second animal running along the ridge, but
it was too dark to fire.

There was nothing for it but to stand still and long for it
to clear. The gun-bearer now came up, and of course got
excited and idiotic, and on its clearing sufficiently to enable us
to see that one stag was looking very feeble, and beyond was
looming the head and horns of the second, the man began to
gesticulate and talk. The clouds would not lift thoroughly, the
head and horns of the stag looked perfectly gigantic through the
mist, and it was only for fear of its getting darker that I fired
at what little I could make out. All this time the wounded stag
was standing in deep snow, with his nose almost touching the
surface, and did not even move, when on running forward to
find out the result of the second shot I came close to him.

Passing him I put a round bullet behind his shoulder, and
then looked for blood-tracks from the second. There was plenty
about, but as to where he was hit I could only conjecture, most
likely on the jaw bone, for the blood was thrown about on either
side of the track. It was very tantalizing, but it was useless to
follow at that time; if camp was reached by nightfall it was
all that could be hoped for.

By daylight we were on the ground, but it was impossible
to war with the elements; sleet and cutting hail were too much
for all of us, and after tracking the wounded beast for a long
distance we gave in. Some days afterwards the stag was seen
and chased by the villagers, but he then escaped, and was not
found until the snow melted.

I once got a stag in a very lucky manner; he was calling in
some dense undergrowth, and I could not see him, although I
was within one hundred and fifty yards. Patiently I sat on
the bank on the other side of the stream. The bushes moved,
and once or twice I caught a glimpse of his antlers. He called
most persistently, and walked about backwards and forwards.
At last I made out a small patch of his hide, and taking a
deliberate pot shot, fired. The animal behaved in a most
extraordinary way, dashing about here and there, but not
making off in any one direction. Whenever I got a glimpse

of him I fired a snap shot. After the fourth shot he was still, and I thought he had got clean away, for I heard no falling sound. The bushes were over my head, and I could scarcely get through them. Suddenly I came right ou the stag sitting on his hind quarters. I was so close that I just missed being upset by a sweep of his horns. It was all over with him, for he was paralyzed. The first shot had hit him fair on the flank, and another bullet had grazed his chest. I can only imagine that he would have made off, but for this second shot, which coming in front had bewildered him. The last bullet had gone through his spine very far back, and he had subsided on to his hind-quarters. He was one of the best ten-pointers I have ever seen.

There are some very good localities for winter-shooting not far from Changus, between Changus and Nowboog village; also in Kotihar, the villages of Dhaupoor and Dardpoora, and the vicinity of Harpatnar and Googaldar. Somewhere near here the Maharajah has a preserve, but although I walked through it, I have forgotten the name of the place. Any way there was nothing in it except a few hinds; but in winter it must be full of stags; it is just the ground to hold Barasingh. Loor holds stags. Keyl, which is six miles from Eshmarkam, is a good place for head-quarters. I can fancy any of the outside hills in the Liddar valley giving very fair sport during a severe snowfall, but of all places I should recommend the Sindh. It is close to Srinaggar which is no small advantage when travelling is difficult; it is a good place for supplies and not by any means bad going. Try the Chittingool ridge ou the Wangut side during a severe winter. The Wangut nullah, as high up as the Wangut village, particularly the Kulnar ravine and the Kutch-numbul hill side, are good if the snow is not *very* deep. Kond, six miles from Islamabad, and beyond that Dandwar, might also be tried. The latter place is good in October. In the spring, when the snow is melting, is, to my idea, far the best time, and I would sooner have from February 20th to March 20th after the stags than all the rest of the year. They are then down on the young green grass, and are busily devouring the crocuses. Under the Margan pass in the Nowboog valley, up the Sindh by Marmar and Gugangair. In the immediate vicinity of Palgaum, and on any of the return tracks from their winter quarters, several heads should be obtained. Naturally the ground leading to where the sportsman wishes afterwards to shoot Ibex or Markhor will be the country he will choose.

Later than March 20th the stags may or may not carry horns. Ou April 6th and 7th I saw quantities of deer near Dubtal under the Margan, but none but the prickets carried horns.

The measurements of the finest heads I have seen are—

Length of horns.	Girth above brow antler.	Divergency at Tips.		Tines.	Where shot.
		Greatest.	Least		
47 inches	7¼ inches	56	20 inches.	13	Sindh Valley.
46 ,,	8 ,,	50	32 ,,	12	Do.

The biggest stag I have seen stood 49½ inches at the shoulder. I never weighed, but one ; I imagine that they are lighter than a Sambhur. The one I did weigh was just 400lbs , and was, I should say, a fair specimen. Average measurements are difficult to give ; some horns are long owing to the length of the terminal snags, and yet are not good handsome heads. Thickness of beam, and well developed points are the chief beauty. No one should despise any well-shaped ten-antlered stag whose horns measure 40 inches.

What constitutes a tine is a disputed point. Deer-stalkers at home count the smallest knot, but false points off a tine, and not off a beam, should surely not be called tines. If they are I have seen many twelve, thirteen, and fourteen-pointers. Any way this stag generally has ten good tines.

Dismal accounts of the destruction of this fine deer have lately reached me from Kashmir. A friend who stayed in the valley during the winter of 1881-82 writes : " I have no great hopes of doing much amongst the stags during the coming calling season. We had very heavy snow in March, and the game was greatly destroyed. In Chittingool and again in Nowboog many deer were slaughtered in the heavy snow, and if this sort of thing continues there will soon be little game left."

It is a great pity that the game should thus be ruthlessly killed, but I do not see what can be done without very stringent game laws ; and stringent laws of this description would be an awful weapon in the hands of a Kashmir petty official.

That these deer will be some day almost unknown in Kashmir there is little doubt ; but it will take many years before it happens.

The country they wander over is very extensive, and is very thinly populated in many parts ; in these two facts lies the safety of the game.

CHAPTER XIII.

THE MUSK DEER (*Moschus moschiferus*).

The Roos or Kustoorah of Kashmir.

THE Musk Deer is more hunted than any other animal that inhabits the Himalaya.

The males, unfortunately for them, are the owners of musk-pods which are worth from Rs. 3 to Rs. 5 even in the jungles ; and this is a sum that is large in the eyes of the villagers. It is, therefore, not a matter of surprise that they are trapped in nooses, or are driven against nets which fall and envelop the bounding animals, as they rush madly against them in their efforts to escape from the men and dogs behind. Coupled with these instruments for destruction, comes the native shikari with his smoothbore, loaded with scraps of iron or with shot, which has been given to him by European visitors. After this, there are its fair and natural enemies—the rifle, the leopard, the wild dog, the pine marten, and the big birds of prey. No wonder that the Musk Deer is now unheard of in places where 15 years ago it was daily to be seen.

This deer is a retiring, forest-dwelling animal, which stands about 22 inches in height, and weighs from 25lbs to 30lbs. Possibly it may have struck others besides myself that the Musk Deer grows to a larger size in our Indian Himalayas than it does in Kashmir, and in the hills bordering on Ladak. The heaviest that I have weighed in these latter places was lighter than any I have met with in the valleys of the Tonse, Jumna and Ganges rivers.

For locality, anywhere in the large forest throughout hills of an elevation exceeding 7,000 feet, there is a chance of the Musk Deer being obtained. It is not an animal much followed by Europeans, but if one or two specimens are required, driving is the surest method of obtaining them. The Wardwan men are the most experienced at this description of sport. Tilail is the best shooting ground ; and any one holding the Gugai ravines is sure to get as many Musk Deer as he requires.

In the forest it is difficult to tell the sexes apart ; the only chance is that of seeing the canine teeth of the male. The shikaris declare that the male, when suddenly startled, makes a hissing sound, and that the female is silent. I do not believe this to be the case ; both sexes, I imagine, sometimes make this noise.

The young are easily reared in a cold climate ; a sheep makes the best foster-mother. It is a mistake when rearing any wild animal under a goat or sheep to overfeed the milk-giver.

I

Gram must never be given, and all grain is better avoided if grass is procurable.

I have mentioned the pine marten (*Martes flavigula*) as an enemy of the Musk Deer. On the Mussoori and Simla road, three of these vermin ran down and killed a half-grown animal within a hundred yards of where I was encamped. Again last year I was watching a Markhor which was standing like a statue on a large block of grey granite, when I spied three or four martens evidently hunting. Looking carefully, I saw a Musk Deer which was working its way up the hill. I did not see the result of the chase as the Markhor took up my attention.

Some years ago, a well-known forest officer and sportsman made a special request that no one would kill Musk Deer in the vicinity of a forest hut, which was situated on a secluded range of hills. For several consecutive years, I was in the habit of shooting pheasants near this hut, and was surprised at the rapidity of the increase of deer. Hodgson tells us that " they grow very rapidly, and can procreate ere they are a year old."

The flesh is not bad venison, but requires to be kept for some time. The whole of the Indian jungle meat requires careful cooking. The Kashmir stag is the best, and if a saddle is kept for ten or twelve days during September or October, and the fat not *all* stolen, it is far from unpalatable. The tongues, slightly salted and smoked, are very good. The soup made from the shin bones is excellent. The marrow-bones are good, and a dish can be made by hashing the kidneys. Spotted Deer shot in December and January supply the same delicacies. Sambhur are uneatable, except the tongue and marrow bones. Barking Deer are fairly good venison. Hog Deer are * * *— well the grubs of the bot fly which infest its skin have prejudiced me against them and also against hares. The Indian hare is much improved by being basted with milk. The Serow and Goral are I consider simply detestable.

Chikara and Antelope are generally shot near a station, and gram-fed mutton and beef are so far preferable that their venison is not often cooked for food. Still I have tasted a very good haunch of black buck.

CHAPTER XIV.

THE BARKING OR RIB-FACED DEER (*Cervulus aureus*.)

In the Pir Panjal, Kakrell; Locally, in Koonjenag, Niboo; The Khakur of the North-west; Muntjar of Central Provinces, generally Jungli Bukra.

VERY few of the Kashmiri shikaris know of the existence of this deer, for it is not found in the valley. It exists in almost all the jungles and hill forests, ranging from the extreme south to an elevation of about 7,000 feet in the Himalayas. It extends to the southern boundaries of Kashmir, Pir Panjal, and Murree hills.

The Khakur is so well known that it seems useless to write a long account of its habits, but it so happens that its pursuit has been a favorite pastime, and has been the cause of a few incidents which may amuse our readers.

A gentleman, who lately wrote to the *Asian*, pointed out an error in the measurements given by Dr. Jerdon of the Khakur's horns. I have only seen one pair of horns 8 inches in length; they came from a temple in Native Ghurwal. Out of sixty specimens I have been lucky enough to get two pairs which exceeded 7 inches.

The largest I have shot were—

Ht. at shoulder.	Weight.	L. of horns.	Where shot.
26 inches	42lbs.	5¼inches	Native Ghurwal.
26 „	37 „	5½ „	Pabar valley. (Himalayas.)
27 .,	44 „	6 „	Central Provinces.
27 „	40 „	7½ „	Kotli Dun.
26 „	37 „	7½ „	Near Mussoori.

A female stood 23 inches and weighed 32lbs.

Out of 32 males shot in the Siwalik hills, not one had horns which exceeded 5¼ inches. Of course the hairy pedicle from which the horn springs is not included in these lengths.

The habit of barking is often fatal to the Khakur, and but for its wonderful aptitude for concealing itself under bushes would lead to its total extermination. Many and many a time have I gone out from my hut or tents when attracted by this sound, and yet not got a shot. A cessation in the noise, then one short bark, a rustle in the bushes, and possibly a glimpse of red hair, and the nimble little beast was gone.

Not long ago, duty was kind enough to take me into the haunts of this game. On a very sultry evening in June, when walking even a few yards was an exertion, the barking of the deer was heard. First came the short sound of the doe Cheetul, then the continuous barking of the Khakur. A man-eater had been reported in the vicinity; could he be about? Walking cautiously along we looked over the brow of a small hill. Bark, bark went the deer, but nothing could be seen. Although inclined to shirk work owing to the intense heat, it seemed a pity to throw away any chance of finding out the tiger's whereabouts.

The parched ground gave no tracks, and at last I sauntered homewards. When near the hut, a servant rushed up and excitedly exclaimed : " The blacksmith has been taken close to the horses' shed." It was too true ; a spot of blood, a shoe and a bit of cloth was all that could be seen. A little further on was another shoe, and a mark of dragging, which extended for a few yards ; then came a space of hard ground which bore no marks whatever.

After looking in every direction it struck me that the tiger must have gone past the Barking Deer ; and if it was after he took the man, there might be a clue. On a bush there was a scrap of the victim's clothes, and then blood was found. About a quarter of a mile from the spot there was a small patch of reeds and swamp, and the chances were, that as the brute had taken that direction, he would go to it, and lie up. The gun-bearer was sent for some fireworks, and to bring up the only elephant that was in camp. Long before he came back I had found the marks leading into the swamp, and after walking all round, had made certain of the tiger being inside. How to get him out was the difficulty. To go in on the elephant would have been of no use ; to beat him out with coolies would have been unfair on the men ; but somehow he must be killed ! At last it was settled that the beaters were to line one side of the swamp and shout ; the elephant with the old gun-bearer was to beat up the reeds, and I was to take up a position on some open ground which lay between the swamp and the hills. It all came off beautifully ; the tiger came out with a rush, and made for the hills, but the Henry Express was too much for him, and he did not travel far. He died like the cur he was, for on following him upon the elephant, he allowed himself to be approached to within twenty yards, and then tried to sneak away. Another tiger was brought to bag by means of a Barking Deer. The little animal barked incessantly and induced my shikari, Old Gunga, to wander about looking for tracks, until success rewarded our efforts.

On the other hand the Barking Deer has done me bad turns. A terrier, which was valuable beyond price, was killed by the tushes of a wounded buck that he was keeping at bay, and a Ghoorka shikari had his hand very badly lacerated when catching a disabled animal.

The wild dog and the leopard prey on the Khakur, and the pine marten destroys the young ones.

In the Siwalik hills near Kalawallah and at Andheri there are plenty of these small deer to be found. In Ghurwal and in parts of Kumaon they are common enough.

The young are difficult to rear, but if reared become very tame. They are not easy to feed, and require a great variety of food.

CHAPTER XV.

THE THIBETAN ANTELOPE (*Kemas Hodgsonii*).
*Nearly all the Shikaris know it as Heran.   The Ladak name is Chiru
and Choos.*

I DO not think the average length of a full grown buck's
horns can be more than 22 inches. Since writing to the
Asian I have again had good opportunities of judging. In
my letter I wrote as follows:—"During a season when antelope were very plentiful in the Changchenmo and the neighbourhood, three sportsmen killed forty-two bucks between
them. Naturally they selected the finest heads to shoot at,
and no single specimen was over 26 inches, and only eight
were 24 inches or over." Since then, in 1881, four guns shot
forty-nine bucks ; and the longest horn was 26½ inches. I
saw all these heads,—in fact many were my own.
The largest I have succeeded in bagging were—

Height.	Weight.	Length of horns,	Where shot.
37 inches.	85lbs.	24 inches.	Under Demjorla.
36 „	85 „	26½ „	Kyam Changchenmo.
37 „	90 „	24 „	Kieu-la.

In one or two books on Ladak shooting the *average* is put
at 27 to 28 inches. I daresay they *sometimes* attain this
length.
The Chiru is only found at high altitudes; the lowest I
have seen it was at 14,800, and the highest between 18,000
and 19,000 feet. From the stony plains between Pamzal and
Kyam up to the Kepsangla (leading into, or rather in Lhassa
territory) up the ravines on the right and left bank of the
Changchenmo, near Gogra, at the head of the Kobrang nullah
and as far east as the Mipal-looma, I can answer for these
antelope being at certain season of the year plentiful. They
are also to be met with on the Karakorum ranges, but how
far beyond I do not know. In June they are very plentiful
near Gogra; in July higher up the ravine is better ground.
During the spring and summer months the sexes keep much
apart. Some nullahs seem only to hold females, notably those
between Kepsang (the one near Radha, *not* the pass) and the
Changchenmo. All I saw under the Changluug in June 1881
were either females or very small bucks. The Kieung-la and
Ning rhi are the best places I know of. (Map, Chap. IX).
The color is a yellowish white, some specimens being of a
reddish hue. The muzzle is dark in color, broad and excessively ugly. The females are hornless and are much smaller than
the males. The coat is more like wool than hair, and at the
time that Europeans generally reach Thibet, the skin is useless,

for the wool comes off at the slightest touch. The skin itself is excessively thin, and tears easily.

The Chiru does not seem to have a very happy time of it, for its skin is perforated by the grubs of a fly, and are found in the spring months in dozens, mostly on the hind quarters. Evidently they are a source of great annoyance to the animal, for the antelopes may often be seen suddenly to rise, and after twitching their hind quarters, to scour over the plains. The Tartars declare that as soon as the animal becomes fat these grubs entirely disappear. The grub does not penetrate into the flesh, and the meat is not at all bad eating. It makes first-rate soup.

The breeding season is later than that of most of the Thibet animals. I saw no young ones before the end of June. Although plentiful, the Thibetan Antelope is very difficult to approach on fairly open ground, and most shots will have to be fired at 250 yards. If the ground is favorable for stalking no difficulty will be met with, but on the ordinary plains it is trying work, crawling along inch by inch. Early in the season, the antelope can sometimes be crawled up to on very open ground, but they will not stand if the sportsman gets on to his hands and knees. The shooter's coat should have double cloth from the elbow to the wrist, and the knees of the knicker-bockers should be patched, or they will wear out, in a very few stalks. Another warning I would give. When pushing the rifle in front be careful that no small pebbles get into the barrel, or a nasty scour down the barrel will be the result when you fire.

This is a sport which palls on one, and after a few days the sportsman is apt to get careless, and not be sufficiently patient. The Tartars declare that this antelope can be approached down wind as easily as against it. Believe it reader if you like, but do not try it often, or you will find yourself turning your back on Changchenmo with one or two pairs of horns instead of having scored ten or a dozen trophies. How many heads you take back depends entirely on the amount of trouble you will give yourself, and on your powers of judging distance. But an average shot, *if patient*, should certainly kill as many specimens as he requires in less than a month, provided that the ground has not been too much shot over during the season.

CHAPTER XVI.

THE THIBETAN RAVINE DEER (*Procapra pecticaudata.*)

The Goa of Thibet; The Gutturosa Antelope.

I CAN tell nothing about this little Antelope beyond what Kinloch has already mentioned. The only country I know of where it is to be met with is near the Tso Morari lake and about Hanle. I have never had the luck to get any good horns; and during a late visit to these parts was debarred from shooting in the vicinity owing to the number of guns already on the ground. The Vizier of Ladak told me that they were still very plentiful, and if I ever wander up there again, I hope to better the trophies I now possess, which are only 11 inches in length.

In 1882 a sportsman, who went from Lahoul to the lake, and from there to Hanle, succeeded in bagging ten Goa in five days; and amongst them were two with horns of 13 inches.

There is another antelope which many of my readers probably never heard of. I give the words of a well-known traveller: "I came on *A. gutturosa* all over Western Mongolia from the northern bend of the Yellow river to the Altai mountains; they were generally in large herds, sometimes I should think four or five hundred or more together. I took home one pair of horns (which I shot just south of the desert) and gave them to Blyth. The Chinese call them 'Hwang Yang or Yellow Goat.' They also exist all over Eastern Mongolia. Major Biddulph shot one 40 or 50 miles west of Maralbashi on the road between there and Kasghar. It is called Djerau there, and Major Biddulph calls it a Gazelle. The buck measures 27½ inches at the shoulder, and the horns are thus described: 'It resembles the Common Indian Gazelle, except that the horns are rather longer, and curve outwards, the tips being turned sharply inwards towards one another.'"

The only way to get horns that I know of, is to induce some trader to bring them down. Blyth classifies the animal as "*A. gutturosa*, sub-genus *Procapra*."

CHAPTER XVII.

THE YAK *(Poephagus gruniens.)*
The Dhong.

THE Dhong of Thibet is to be met with in only few places which are open for the European sportsman to wander over. It is easy enough to find a considerable number of cows and calves, but nearly all the big males leave the Thibet shooting grounds before Europeans can reach those parts.

I *may* have helped some few people to obtain other hill game, but I do not hoax myself with the idea that I can do much towards aiding in the obtaining of bull Yak. Kinloch has already told us of his difficulties and ultimate success. I cannot add much; by all means try the Kobrang, or as the maps have it, the Kugrang. If this fails, go up the Kiepsang. This place is about eight miles from Kyam. The hunter should try the heads of all the branch ravines. He is certain to see cows if he is the first on the ground.

It is quite three or four to one against any individual sportsman getting a big bull on any single trip.

Now for hearsay. A gentleman, who has twice been to the locality, when on his way to Yarkand, said to me: "Why do you waste your time in the neighbourhood of the Changchenmo; go to Kizil Jilgha." I fully intended to take his advice and went as far as the dreary Lingzinthung plains, but circumstances prevented me from continuing the journey.

Beyond the fact that there is no fuel nor grass for some six or seven marches, there would appear to be no other difficulties. Owing to this want of fodder, it is *absolutely necessary* to take ponies for baggage animals beyond Shumal Longpa, for Yaks will not eat grain, and although they will eat barley meal cakes in small quantities they will not travel far when fed only on this food.

The trip to the Karakash could easily be done from Gogra in eight or nine days, and I should advise some enterprising spirit to try it. All the heavier baggage might be left at Gogra where the Yaks could graze during the traveller's absence, and a hurried march to the Karakash and back with a fortnight on the shooting ground could easily be accomplished.

Gogra to Shumal Longpa is about twelve miles. Over the Changlung Burma pass, which is at an elevation of 19,280 feet above the sea according to the maps, but must surely be lower, is a long day's journey. Then it is a dreary walk on the other side to where Nischu is marked. On the fourth day I was told to camp on the plains, and if possible to do 20 miles. On the fifth day I was to go to the vicinity of some salt lakes; and then one or two more days should land the traveller on his shooting grounds, or at any rate at the Kizil pass.

The route taken by Major Biddulph is mentioned in Col. Gordon's "Roof of the World."

My informant seemed perfectly certain that I should find Yak bulls on the banks of the Karakash, but although inclined to believe the story myself, I can only vouch for what I have seen. Once again, here is more hearsay : At Shipki an enterprising Tartar assured me that he could take me over the frontier and show quantities of bull Yak. I have so often been dragged about with the promise of bulls and showu only cows that I felt very little inclination to try, and the demanded reward moreover was too high. From either Niti or by the Rudok route, I feel perfectly certain that any European would be turned back. The Rudok men watch the Kepsangla. I do not believe in their doing the traveller any personal injury, but if the inhabitants met a European, they would insist on his return.

There are, however, so very few people about, that if marches were made over the hills, and not on regular tracks, in all probability no one would be met with ; of course it would be much better for two friends to try it together.

On one occasion, when I was over the frontier, a body of Tartars who were insisting on another traveller's return said : "We know there is another Sahib about, but we have not seen him, and consequently it is no business of ours ; but if we once meet a Sahib, and let him proceed on his journey, the headmen of Rudok will kill us." Of course the Englishman had to return, and when he announced his intention of giving in they were civil enough. There is no doubt that the Tartars who drive the traveller's Yaks deliberately urge the others to turn the camp back; they hate having to go far, and if anything did happen to an Englishman, they would have a very poor time of it with the Leh authorities.

Formerly there was an easy route over the Kharnak ford into the eastern end of the Changchenmo, but now it is watched. The maps call the place a ford, but it is far too deep to wade through, and a raft has to be made. Wonderful to relate, there is sufficient wood in the place to make a raft, but if the Tartars come before it is complete, they can easily stop the crossing.

Jerdon gives the measurements of two bulls' heads. His larger one was 30 inches long by 15 inches in circumference. The largest one I have seen was slightly longer ; it was shot in 1869, and the bull was measured as seventeen and a half hands at the shoulder. The cows are not worth shooting after the month of April, for the hair all falls out, and the tail is the only trophy. The horns are very poor indeed.

K

Tails, if wanted, can be bought in Leh, and in many of the Himalayan villages for a trifle, so that it certainly is not worth while to shoot a cow.

A solid bullet from a ·500 Express will be found heavy enough for Yak, and on the off chance of meeting this game it is not worth while to carry a big bore rifle.

What success would attend staying in Changchenmo during November I cannot say ; there seems no very great difficulty in the way. It would, under ordinary circumstances, be possible to leave that valley as soon as the rivers were frozen over even supposing the Marsemik was closed, but I am not certain about getting out the baggage.

The Changla would, in all probability, be closed, but I cannot imagine the Marsemik being an unsurmountable obstacle. Once over the Marsemik, there is a route by Shyok village over the Diga-la which is always open.

A whole winter in the highlands of Ladak would be too terrible to think of; besides it would be useless discomfort ; but in the late autumn months, the Yaks' skins would be in really splendid order. The bull's hide with the hair in good condition is an infinitely finer trophy than are the horns.

CHAPTER XVIII.

THE KYANG OR WILD ASS OF THIBET (*Equus himionus.*)

As an animal to be shot at in the way of sport, I do not include the Kyang, but it is sometimes necessary to shoot one to satisfy the Tartars' craving for meat. Again the skins make excellent coverings for kiltas and soles for the servants' shoes.

They are met with near the Pangong lake, and are very common in many parts. I have seen them not far from Gya. When stalking in the Changchenmo, they are sometimes troublesome, and twice have put up Ovis Ammon that I was approaching, and several times have startled Antelope and Burhel.

The hoofs are occasionally brought back, and made up into inkstands and paper weights.

I have found the remains of Kyang which have been eaten by wolves, and a gentleman of my acquaintance came on five wolves whilst they were engaged in gorging themselves on a full-grown Kyang. What a race the wild ass must have had for its life!

I never heard of a Kyang being broken to saddle, but they can be made tolerably tame. One was feeding on the banks of the Indus in company with some of the Vizier's ponies when I passed through Leh in 1881.

CHAPTER XIX.

THE BEARS (BLACK AND BROWN) (*Ursus tibetanus* and *U. isabellinus*.)

THE Black Bear or the Harput of Kashmir is steadily decreasing in numbers in the happy valley. There are more to be found in our own territory, in Ghurwal, and in Chumba, and in some other parts of the Himalayas than are now to be seen in Kashmir.

Black Bears are easily shot, and there is no reason why any hardships should be endured in the pursuit of them; consequently nearly every visitor goes in for a shot at Bruin.

Although they are decreasing in numbers, the bears are still sufficiently common for a few to fall yearly to the rifles of most men who care to pursue them. The sport is, however, very poor, and there is little excitement in it as they seldom fight. The majority killed are shot in walnut and apple trees, and in the Indian corn fields.

The fur is at its best in November, when the Black Bear may sometimes be shot in the hawthorn trees; but it is very difficult to carry out a stalk at that season, owing to the dryness of the fallen leaves and the slipperiness of the grass. It is however one of the few amusements left after the stags have ceased calling, and the snow has not yet fallen.

Fruit of various kinds, honey, grubs and corn are the usual food, but carrion is also greedily eaten.

Some of the males are very large. One measured was six feet six inches in length, but most are under six feet. A very fine bear skin from the Lolab when tanned was six feet four inches long by four feet across the back, and five feet over the hind quarters. The females are much smaller, and unless barren seldom have good coats.

From March 15th to May 15th are the only months in the season that the hair is still in condition, so that the majority of the visitors to the valley are obliged to get a good skin during that time, or not at all. In the Lower Himalayas the various oaks produce acorns in the autumn months; one description fruits in November; and as our own hills are not then so dry, numbers of bears are to be shot in the trees; Kurna and Justun in Jonsar Barwar, about four marches from Mussoori, are very good spots to visit.

Almost any Kashmir shikari is capable of taking the sportsman up to bears, or of driving them out of the jungles, if sufficient help is supplied by the villagers. So that I shall conclude by simply naming a few places, any of which are sure to yield a skin or two.

The Lolab valley. Throughout the hills near Baramulla in the Hammel pergunnah, these are a sure find in the apple season; the best villages to camp at are those on the north side of the mountains, and there is a good road from Dobgaum. This place is on the Jhelum between Baramulla and Sopoor. The Bundipoora nullah is the next best place. The Sindh valley as high as Goond, the favorite spots are opposite Kangan on the left bank of the river at Rezin and the lower portions of Wangut ravine; in the autumn try above Nuna. In Nowboog valley. The hazelwoods of Lidroo and above Palgaum in the Liddar. The northern slopes of Gulmurg as far as Shupyan.

The Brown Bear is the Harput or Lal Balu of Kashmir shikaris and the Drinmor of Ladakis. It is much more worthy of pursuit than is the black variety. It is true that it is easily approached if stalked against the wind, and seldom fights, but from October 15th to May 15th it carries a splendid coat.

The Brown Bear hibernates for a longer period than the black. Few are to be seen about after December 1st. It emerges from its winter retreat early in April, and may then be seen digging in the snow, and endeavouring to find the bodies of ibex which have been overwhelmed in avalanches, but oftener it is viewed on some southern slope, when engaged in searching for earth-nuts and the roots of grasses, or in turning over loose stones, and greedily licking up the grubs concealed beneath. In November, the spots where sheep have been folded during the summer are certain to reward the sportsmen.

They have been shot very low down in Hammel (See Map Kajnag, Chap. IV), but as a rule are not found at a less altitude than 8,000 feet. Jerdon mentions one as being $7\frac{1}{2}$ feet in length. I cannot go near this measurement, although I have seen as many as most men, and thought I had got an enormous one when the tape showed 6 feet 10 inches. I would feel inclined to put the average male at 6 feet or a few inches over at the most, but 1 am aware that many men give a far greater length. I have been supplied with some measurements of Bears killed in Chumba, but must decline to give them, although I am sure they are supposed to be *bonâ fide*. However, I believe from what I have seen, that the bears run to a large size in that state.

In years gone by twenty to thirty bears often fell to one gun, but now-a-days half that number is a good season's bag, if taken in conjunction with other game.

For localities, Shamshibri, then northwards to Shardi and Gumot nullahs. Up the Kishengunga are Keyl, Foulwein, and Gugai, Gurais and Tilail. South-east from Tilail try Dras and Zogila. Lidarwat and Pangitarni, lying towards the sacred caves of Amarnath. Crossing over the passes drop into

the Sunyan valley and follow it down to Sooknis; then
through the Wardwan, and after that the famous Ibex nullahs
Krishnye and Znisnye, and I think I have selected the best
places. I might include the Tosh-a-maidan, but the Pir range,
although holding bears, cannot be compared with the other
localities mentioned (Map, Chap. XII). In Chumba try
Manglee, Kilar, &c., but my knowledge of those parts is not
very recent.

CHAPTER XX.

THE LEOPARD (*Felis pardus*).

THE Leopard is a perfect nuisance; it destroys game, and worse than that, is always on the look-out to catch dogs.

It should be, I uphold, destroyed in every possible way— by trapping, by sitting over baits and by driving. The means of destruction will form the subject of this chapter.

Trapping can be done in two ways, either by employing various kinds of cage-traps, or else by means of gins.

The best cage-trap is that which is often employed by the Ghoorkas. This can be made either double or single, that is, with one or two entrances. A suitable spot would be where the bleating of the kid, which is to be used for a bait, can be heard on all sides.

The place being chosen, drive into the ground two parallel rows of stakes; if for a double trap, each row to be 11 feet long; for a trap with single entrance, $6\frac{1}{2}$ feet will suffice.

The space between the two parallel rows should be about 18 inches wide, and the distance between the stakes not more than two or three inches. The stakes should stand 24 inches above ground, and be driven in very firmly.

In the centre, stake off a compartment, two feet in length to hold the kid. In other words you have two traps, each $4\frac{1}{2}$ feet long, and in the centre, a compartment two feet square. Fasten above these two larger compartments cross or top pieces of wood; these must be firmly spiked down on to the upright stakes. Next come the doors, which must be of boards, not less than $1\frac{1}{2}$ inch thick. The doors are set with a catch exactly like that of a rat-trap.

Where the bait is usually fixed, instead of a hook, fasten two strong cross wires at right angles to one another. The Leopard springs the trap by trying to get at the goat past the wires, which obstruct the way. Some traps have a board so fixed on the floor of the trap that on the animal treading on it the door descends. The door must be well weighted to ensure its falling quickly. The kid is put into the centre compartment and the top is closed either by a large flat stone, or a board on which stones are piled.

The less finish there is the better; the bark can be left on the stakes, and the ground should not be dug nor disturbed more than is possible. In order to prevent the Leopard from getting on the trap, place over it thorn bushes or boughs. If the kid or puppy, or whatever is used as a bait, is to be sacrificed, there is no necessity to make a centre compartment; but if a double entrance is made, it is better to shut it off for it is not easy to ensure both doors being simultaneously dropped.

Now and again an unwary Leopard has been caught in a gigantic box-trap.

Gins are difficult to arrange, and my experience points out that they are seldom successful, whereas the rough cage-trap very often is.

In the neighbourhood of the Kashmir villages, the Leopards can be shot over goats, and a few are thus yearly obtained below Gulmurg.

In the winter all the Leopards are down near the villages, but in the summer many follow the sheep on to their grazing grounds high up amongst the mountains.

The neighbourhood of Islamabad is much frequented by these animals. The shikaris call them "Cheetah," and are all sufficiently well up in their work to make the necessary arrangements. I may, therefore, dismiss the common Leopard and turn our attention to the animal that all sportsmen call the Snow Leopard or Safed Cheetah.

(*Felis uncia*).

In Thibet "*Stian.*"

The places where there is the best chance of obtaining this animal are in the Nubra valley, the road to which lies through Leh. Now and again specimens are obtained from various parts of Ladak. From Soroo I have seen several skins brought down and have come on the Ounce in the Krishnye, and again not far from Tankse. I do not consider it a very rare animal, but it is exceedingly difficult to come across. They prey greatly on the Ibex and Burbel, and on one occasion I had the luck to see one stalking a solitary buck Ibex. It was on the snow, and among huge blocks of ice that had fallen into the valley from the glacier above. The animals were a long distance from me, and had to be watched through a telescope. The stalker failed, and the Ibex went off. Unluckily I had no goat to tie up and never saw the Ounce again. I remember thinking that the animal seemed all tail, and, therefore, concluded it was a male. It may not be generally known that in the males the spots are generally closer together, even blotchy, especially down the spine; the tail longer, heavier and thicker at the end than that of the female. There is also more hair under the throat, and about the jaws. The skin of the female is generally smaller than that of the male, the markings more open, and has more of the white ground exposed, while the tail is shorter and more pointed than in the male.

It is quite a matter of chance getting a shot at an Ounce. A gentleman of my acquaintance shot one without having an idea that he had done anything out of the common. In fact, when telling his list of game, he omitted it entirely. It was his first trip in the Himalayas.

The footprints of the Ounce are often to be seen in many of the more remote nullahs of the Maharajah's dominions, but, as I before said, it is quite a chance to fluke one.

The dimensions given by Dr. Jerdon, page 101, seem to me very large, but my personal acquaintance with the Ounce is limited.

Skins, more or less mutilated, can generally be purchased in Srinaggar at from twenty to thirty rupees; and now and again for a much smaller sum in Leh.

I once saw two young cubs and bid high for their purchase. They had been in captivity for some weeks and were fairly tame. The owner would not part with them at what I could afford to give out of the amount I had put aside for travelling expenses, and he would not, or could not understand the value of a cheque. The cubs have been brought down by European sportsmen, on one, if not on more occasions.

A curious and slightly sensational story is the following:—
A Himalayan traveller, an American, was sitting up watching over some bones of a goat, for nothing else remained of the body. He had won the toss for shot, and was very keen, although neither he nor his companion thought that there was more than the most remote chance of the Snow Leopard turning up. Just before the darkness set in, the animal appeared close to the remains of the goat. The hill side was steep, but the bones were lying on a very small, but tolerably flat place; on receiving the bullet the Ounce bounded downwards, and fell dead on to the shikari below (a Kashmiri) whose howls and shouts were indeed wonderful.

To give the Kashmir shikari his due, he is generally tolerably plucky, but on this occasion his feelings were too much for him.

A European traveller coming through Nubra, saw five Snow Leopards together; imagine his feelings when he got none.

CHAPTER XXI.

THE THIBET LYNX (*Felis isabellina*). THE " EE."

I HAVE never seen a single wild specimen, and only two in captivity, but was much struck with the heavy look of the animal. The Vizier of Ladak had one in perfect health, and took it down as a present to the Maharajah of Kashmir. It was vicious to strangers, and must have been a troublesome companion on the line of march.

Kinloch describes the animal he shot, and has given us a photograph of a stuffed specimen. It is beyond my power to tell any one where he has the best chance of coming on a Thibet Lynx. I saw a skin which the Tartar Yak-drivers had got near Man, on the Pangong lake ; and another was brought to me for sale when I was in Tankse.

The Jungle Cats found in Kashmir are not worth describing. There is, however, a Lynx-like Cat which is found close to Srinaggar, and the skins are offered for sale either singly or made into rugs. The merchants who make up the rugs say that they are the skins of the female jackal! Where this extraordinary idea originated I cannot possibly imagine.

There are also wild cats to be found in the Wardwan and elsewhere, the skins of which can be purchased in the Srinaggar shops for a trifle. The common grey cat skin, sold by the *mochees*, is called *Van Bili*, and if in its winter fur, makes very fair rugs.

CHAPTER XXII.

THE WOLVES AND WILD DOGS OF LADAK AND KASHMIR.

(Canis laniger). The Grey Wolf of Thibet. The Chanko.

THE Chanko is tolerably common in many parts of Thibet, and often proves a great pest to the shepherds, and is considerably in the way of the sportsman. Game will not stay in the nullah if wolves or wild dogs are about, and if their marks are to be seen it is better to give the place a wide berth, and to march away to undisturbed ground. It is, however, the duty of every true sportsman to endeavour to kill off these vermin, but it is not an easy thing to accomplish.

The Tartar shepherds trap the Wolves in pits. They simply dig a pit, leaving the sides vertical, and put in a young goat as a bait. The Wolves jump down and gorge themselves on the wretched animal, and are unable to get out again.

Whether the black Wolf of Thibet, the "Hakpo Chanko" of the Tartars, is a separate species or not it is very difficult to say. Many look on it as an instance of melanism. It doubtless crosses with the common Chanko, for I have seen a grey cub with a black mother, and recorded the fact in the *Asian.* Colonel Kinloch very kindly replied to a letter of mine, and also wrote home and ascertained that all the cubs produced by the pair he gave to the "Zoo" were black. Another writer in the *Asian* describes having seen grey and black Wolves together. The only black Wolf I have seen was, I consider, much larger than the ordinary grey Wolf.

It is not my task to discuss the question, so I leave it after stating what I have seen, and turn to the Wild Dog.

The Wild Dog is tolerably common in Tilail, and less so in the eastern end of the valley. The Kashmiris call them Ram Hun, hun being the Kashmiri for a dog. The Wild Dog is widely distributed over the greater portion of India, and is fairly common in most parts of the Himalayas with which I am acquainted. Years ago, I shot two Wild Dogs out of a pack which were gorging themselves on a Sambhur hind. The dogs did not seem to notice my approach. I did not measure them very carefully, but see on reference to my notes that a male was five feet long including the tail, and I have never seen one larger.

One winter, when shooting in the hills, I was completely puzzled by the entire absence of game in certain ravines where it was nearly always to be found. I wasted several days of my precious leave looking about everywhere. My shikari was indefatigable, and at last found traces of Wild Dogs. The next day I saw three dogs running a Musk Deer. I tried hard to get the vermin, but could not succeed.

Once when lying in camp, lamed by an accident, I heard some Wild Dogs hunting on the hills above. It was in the Siwaliks; and I was waiting impatiently to get a boot on my foot, and to be off after the Sambhur. My old shikari remarked: "It is no use, we will take the elephant up the ravines, and you will see that the game has all run across the main 'rao' (as the dry rivers are called in those parts), and in the opposite direction from where the dogs were hunting." This was done, and the old man's words proved to be rue.

All wild dogs appear to be very shy, and but few are killed.

I do not believe it is possible to tame the young; the ones I had were very vicious, and I could make nothing out of them. They fed well, and gave but little trouble when left alone. I was very glad to give them away, for more unsatisfactory pets I never possessed.

I do not credit the stories of their killing tigers, but I quite believe that they drive them away from the jungles indirectly; for no game stops where Wild Dogs are hunting, and the tigers leave in order to find deer to kill.

In 1873 I was in the Siwalik hills, and had heard of a mare being killed by a tiger. I was unable to go the same morning, and in the afternoon, on reaching the spot where the mare had been dragged, I found the kill had been pulled about and much eaten; and by it lay the bodies of two half-grown Wild Dogs. I watched by the carcase, but nothing ever came. I can but conclude that the tiger destroyed the dogs.

Two of these animals took up their abode close to a village on the banks of the Powra river in Kashmir. They frequently came down into the open country, and harried the sheep. A resident in the neighbourhood tried on one or two occasions to ride them down, but they got away with the greatest ease. This was very unlike the usual shy behaviour of Wild Dogs.

CHAPTER XXIII.

THE SAMBHUR (*Rusa Aristotelis.*)

In the North-West called the Maha; in the hills, Jerow, and erroneously the Bara-Singh.

IN order to complete his collection of horns, the sportsman often wanders far in the pursuit of this stag. There are numberless places where Sambhur are to be found, but it is far from easy to get a good head. I once had the luck to secure a splendid trophy. In March 1867 I was sauntering towards camp after a day's beating in the Rewah district. My feelings were at a very low ebb, for it was rather warm, and I had just missed a tiger. On my right was a pad elephant, which was employed in beating some grass which bordered the open glade along which I walked. The mahout shouted out to me that a Sambhur was coming; it was over in no time; the stag fell at once to the shot, and as he was struggling to rise, a second shot floored him outright. He had the finest head I have secured. I see the entry in my note book gives—

Ht. at shoulder.	Lt. of horns.	Girth of horns above brow antler.	Where killed.
53 inches.	44 inches.	9 inches.	Rewah, C. P.

I have seen some very good heads in the North-West, and one or two real beauties from Nahun territory, but the general run are smaller than those in the Central Provinces.

During my long sojourn in the Siwaliks, I have come on a great number of Sambhur. I also have had my share of the shooting in the Terai, the Kotli and Patli Duns, all of which hold Sambhur, and I think that if I wanted to secure one or two fair heads, and had not command of elephants and camels, and all the paraphernalia of a big camp, that I should bring my small tents down with me from the hills, and rail to Saharunpur. There, I should hire mules or ponies for carriage, and go out to Mohun dâk bungalow. From there I should go to Dolkund, one march towards Hurdwar, and then up into the higher Siwalik hills.

In the Siwaliks, where the Jumna cuts its way through, several ravines run straight down to the river; all these hold Sambhur. Again the Rajah of Nahun has in his territory some good spots for driving this game. With patience these places must yield a trophy or two; and I do not wish to aid any one to go in for indiscriminate slaughter.

The following is an extract from my diary which will prove that, although scarcer, Sambhur are still to be found by those who will work hard, and in places which are tolerably easy to get at.

February 3rd, 1880.—Went out very early, and watched the sun rise when not far from Mohun bungalow. Saw a small Sambhur, fired and missed. Shortly after saw a big one, but did not get a shot.

February 6th.—Got shots at two stags, dropped one with a bullet through the spine, and rolled the other over, but lost him. Gunga displaced a stone above me, and as it fell on my foot, I was unable to do any more walking.

February 13th.—Since the 6th I was unable to stalk. Went out from camp, and saw a really fine stag, but I made a mess of the stalk.

February 14th.—Saw the stag again; but could not get near him. Still very lame.

February 19th.—Shot the stag. I fancy the same I saw on 13th and 14th.

February 21st.—Hit a stag as it was going over the crest of a hill, and afterwards secured him.

Now I maintain that this is quite sufficient sport to satisfy any one. It occurred in the Siwaliks, and I was working under great disadvantages as I was more or less lame after February 6th. The Sambhur generally have cast their horns by April, hence but few good heads fall to the lot of military men whose leave commences on April 15th. I have seen horns in velvet as late as the middle of October, but I think by October 1st the tips are often tolerably firm, although the horns may still have velvet on them.

Tigers are answerable for the death of many a stag, and on several occasions I have picked up good horns from kills. I cannot call to mind having secured any good stags when beating with a large line of elephants. Stalking is much better fun, and more likely to yield fine trophies. Hinds are often put up out of the long grass in a drive, and are frequently quite bewildered and stare up at the elephants. It is a great shame to shoot them; but I am sorry to say it is too often done, though it is quite beyond me to understand what fun can be got out of shooting a Sambhur hind. It might possibly be necessary to do it for the sake of the hide once or twice in a lifetime, but I could tell queer stories about hinds being shot in the Kumaon district, and left to rot on the ground. I would appeal to the good feelings of all brother sportsmen. The shooting ground is getting more and more curtailed in area year by year, and this slaughter is done mostly by young men, often through thoughtlessness, but sometimes out of sheer wantonness. Remember that Sambhur are not prolific; they seldom have more than one fawn, and that it is four years before the young stag assumes his complete shape of horn, and that he has still three or four years to live before he can have a pair of antlers worth preserving. He has quite sufficient chances against his attaining an age of seven or eight years, without having to run the risk of being shot down by the rifle bullet whilst still in his immature state.

Large herds are seldom seen in these days ; but I know one or two very little frequented forest reserves where quantities of Sambhur are harboured, and where doubtless they increase and spread into the neighbouring forests. Dr. Jerdon remarks that the horns rarely exceed 40 inches ; this is, I should say, certainly the case, but it is not at all rare to obtain heads within one or two inches of this measurement.

Sambhur leather is greatly in request for leggings and boots. It can often be purchased in Saharanpur. The great difficulty is to keep the leather soft and pliant, for when once thoroughly wetted, it is apt to become stiff and brittle on drying. I have tried every recipe I can get hold of, but have never been quite successful. The nearest approach to a satisfactory treatment was by putting on the boots, before wearing them, a composition as follows :—one part resin, one part wax, two parts fat, four parts linseed oil *by weight*.

This was applied when warm. The recipe is not my own, and was given me by a friend.

I look upon Sambhur meat as being quite uneatable ; the venison seems to be always tough. Some of the Terai men will not eat the flesh. I cannot imagine why, unless they confuse the animal with the Blue Bull. The Blue Bull or Nilghai is in many places sacred, in fact most natives consider it to be a cow ; and many high caste shikaris are greatly disgusted at seeing one shot. I think I have now completed the list of game likely to be followed by the visitor to Kashmir and Northern India. If the object is to obtain specimens of other game he can consult several books, and will have to invoke the aid of friends ; for it is not easy for every one to get up a line of elephants, nor is it always possible for the sportsman to secure carriage and supplies. In the various places I have mentioned, a great variety of the Indian game can be shot, for the Siwaliks hold Spotted Deer. The Kotli and Patli Duns hold four-horned Antelope and Hog Deer, as well as the game found in the Siwaliks. Both tracts of country hold the Black Bear (*Ursus labiatus*), Tiger and Leopard. Rarely a Lynx is come on, but I have twice seen them in the Dehra Dun. The Eastern Dun is much shot out, but across the Ganges some tracts of country still afford a refuge to the deer and other wild animals. Tigers are tolerably plentiful, but are very wary, and are year by year penetrating further into the Himalayas. On the road under the hills between Laldang and the entrance to the passes into the Kotli and Patli Duns, Nilghai are met with.   There remain now only few specimens of Indian game which I have not touched on.

I have of late years seen but few Swamp Deer (*Rucervus duvancelli*).   They have become much rarer in the forests of Nepal, through which Europeans can sometimes obtain leave to wander, and I have not visited the Central Province shooting grounds for so many years that I cannot give any accurate information, but I saw some fair heads which had been shot in and near the Mandla district in 1879 and 1880.

The measurements of the best head I have seen shot are :—

Length round curve.	Girth of beam above brow antler.	Greatest divergency of tips.	Least divergency of tips.
36½ inches.	6 inches.	32 inches.	20 inches.

I have heard of much bigger heads. Of Antelope I have seen a pair 27¾ inches long, and of Chikara a pair of a little over 14 inches.   The big Antelope's head was from Jeypore ; but I do not know where the Chikara came from.   I have obtained two or three pairs of Chikara horns slightly under this measurement.

Antelope and Chikara (*G. Bennetii*) are common near many of our plains stations.   From the vicinity of some of the railway stations near Allyghur, Black Buck can be obtained. From Hattrass station there is a road running down to the Ganges, along which they are still common, but are yearly getting wilder.

CHAPTER XXIV.

The small game shooting in Kashmir—Some general remarks on the Himalayan small game.

PROBABLY there is no place so completely a failure in the results to be obtained from following small game as Kashmir. The list of birds to be found is a long one, but except the Chikore shooting, which is fairly good, there is nothing worth considering as sport.

Monaul are scattered about the various hill-sides, and in the autumn months are easily found, but are generally very wild.

Above Luchiepoora in the Kaj-nag, there are a good many to be seen. In the Wardwan there are a few. In the Gweenye I have seen as many as six or eight cock birds during a day's walk.

Above Praslang in the Liddar I have come on them frequently when they have been busy digging and scratching on the old sheep folds. I saw a few *near* Maru, and a fair sprinkling of birds in the Sindh. In fact they are everywhere in the higher forests, but except in the Kaj-nag, nowhere really plentiful.

The prices asked for Monaul skins in Srinaggar are ludicrously high, but very few are offered for sale, a conclusive proof that they are not easy to obtain.

The Argus (as it is called) is rare. The Kashmiris call it the Rang Rawal and Danadar. The vicinity of the Murgan and Hoksar are said to be the best places. I saw only one there, but I heard the peculiar quack-like call on several occasions.

The Koklass, or as it is sometimes called the Kukrola, is found everywhere. In the Pir and Kaj-nag there are quantities of these birds. They are very fairly good eating if they have not been feeding on the pine seeds. During the winter I could have shot a good many if I had not been short of gun cartridges; as it was, I succeeded in getting a few with round bullets fired from a ·360 Express.

The Cheer Pheasant I have not met with in Kashmir territory. In parts of our own Himalayas it is plentiful. It is a first-rate table bird, and affords pretty shooting. I once caught a couple of young ones and kept them for a long time in an aviary. They lived through two hot seasons, and were in excellent plumage.

The Kaleege is not known to most of the Kashmir shikaris, but is shot on the Pir route, and near Uri, Tindala, and other places on the Murree road. The Ram Chikore is found on all the loftier hills, but it generally comes on when the sports-

M

man is out after Ibex ; so is left unmolested. It is not a very
good bird to eat. I have seen large numbers in Ladak, and
used to pot them in the early mornings. They carry off a
lot of shot. At Ning Rhi there were any number of these
birds ; but north of the Changchenmo river I rarely saw
them,—in fact I cannot call to mind having killed any in those
parts.

The Chikore shooting in September is good. I have never
made a big bag nor heard of any, but with a spaniel any
reasonably good shot should pick up five or six brace in a
morning's walk. In midwinter they are much poached ; a
shield of the Wild Cat's or Leopard's skin is made and pushed
in front of the gun. The birds congregate together, and the
shikari lets fly into the middle of them.

The best places for Chikore are Awantipore and round the
adjacent hills to Middar, Batgoond, Seer, and as far as Pastooni.
Also above Pampoor, or rather above Khrew. The Maharajah
preserves the ground near the Srinaggar vineyards, but beyond
in the Brain direction there are a few birds. Above Manasbal,
and also above the vineyards at Lar, there are a quantity of
Chikore, but the thorns are very troublesome. (Map, Chap. XII)

Up the Liddar, about 13 miles from Bijbehara, there is a de-
tached hill at Kotsoo. In October it teems with birds and can
be easily driven. I once got 17 birds out of one drive, but the
place is very small, and by the next day I had shot it out, taking
away 22 brace in the two days. I went back after the crops
were cleared away and saw but few.

In Hammel there are Chikore not far from Baramoola. About
two miles up the river, on the right bank, there are plenty
of birds in the early part of the season, viz., September 1st
to 15th, but in the autumn and winter absolutely none.

There are doubtless several other places as good as most
I have mentioned, but I have not tried to find them, as those
named supplied sufficient sport. Kewnus on the Woolar, and
above on the hills near the Shokardin Ziarat did not come up
to the reputation I had heard so much of.

In Ladak there are a good many Sandgrouse; on the far
side of the Kieula they are absurdly tame. Once when shooting
simply for the pot I got five brace in four shots, but of course
my only object was a supply of food with as little firing as
possible. How good these birds were, after tinned beef, tinned
soup, in fact tinned everything.

There are a variety of Pigeons in Ladak and Kashmir, but
except when marching along the Leh road, I seldom molested
them.

Woodcock are found here and there. A few solitary Snipe
and a few Jack are to be picked up ; but Snipe-shooting in the
valley cannot compare with our Indian sport; one or two

fair bags are however yearly made near Sumbul. In winter there are endless wild fowl on the big lakes, but they are very difficult to approach; by rising before the mist is off the water, and standing on the edge of the lake, a choke bore will generally bring to bag a few Geese and Mallards. Nothing but a punt gun is of any use on Woolar lake. Near Sumbul there are two jheels which I have seen literally covered with duck, but I never could get near them, and used to consider myself lucky if I bagged three or four birds. Teal are to be got at on the Anchar lake, also on various pools and streams, and in midwinter on Manasbal.

The fact is, the wild fowl get into the open water during the day, and at night go to their feeding grounds. Flight shooting can be practised on the Dal lake and on the shores of the Woolar, but if the sportsman has been accustomed to really good duck-shooting in India, he will probably not get enough shots to satisfy him. Every boatman has a gun, and it is a regular case of file firing all day long. The wretched birds have no peace anywhere. During a very severe winter, when the big lakes and the Jhelum are blocked with ice, there must be plenty of wild-fowl-shooting, but, as I have before remarked, it must be very difficult to get about during such a season.

In British territory there is really some very pretty shooting to be obtained in the Himalayas. Far be it from me to help the Monaul destroyers in any way; they have done damage enough, and but for our reserved forests, the bright-plumaged game birds bid fair to become extinct. Not long ago in a Government forest I counted no less than nineteen cock Monaul during one morning's walk. Five years ago there were scarcely any; but before the mania for bright feathers set in, it was easy to get six or seven brace of Pheasants, of which three or four birds would be Monaul on any winter's day in these woods.

I could not very well mention better places for Pheasant-shooting than I have done, when speaking of various animals, such as the Gooral, &c. I have never tried to make a bag of Pheasants, so that what I have done should not be taken as what could be done. It so happens that I have spent several winters in the Himalayas and have only shot what I required. Often there was no one to give the birds to, and I have always had a great admiration for them, and felt unwilling needlessly to destroy them. Chikore have, however, been the exception to this rule. Day after day have I toiled after them, and never have I got beyond a bag of ten or twelve brace. They are the most aggravating creatures in existence; they spoil one's dogs, and regularly tire one out; but still they afford splendid exercise, and it is a very triumphant feeling, when, during some morning's walk, one has scored against them. Chikore are very fond of yew berries, and their little weakness told strongly against them on one occasion when I was encamped on a ridge. I could not give up much time to the birds, but I did square a few accounts during those ten days.

As I before remarked Hume and Marshall's book has so lately come through the Press that a long dissertation on Game Birds would be useless. Pheasants and Partridges, both rare and common, are there fully described. I have, therefore, almost entirely confined my remarks on small game to what may be found in Kashmir; and have purposely omitted one or two of the rare species, as the visitor will probably not come across them; and if he does, can find them out in the book referred to.

In Ladak the small game is very useful in helping out one's limited cuisine; and none more so than are the hares. There are several varieties to be found, and they are all first-rate eating; not nearly so dry and insipid as the Indian animal. There are hundreds of hares under the Marsemik pass in some of the Gya nullahs, and also near Shooshal. Hares are found at Gilgit, and in endless other places. They afford very pretty shooting with a pea rifle, when the sportsman is loth to disturb his shooting ground by frequent discharges of his shot gun.

Mr. Sterndale has given us a long list of the various hares. Before perusing it I had no idea there were so many species and I expect but few men had.

CHAPTER XXV.

Hints on preserving horns and skins from decay.

ALL the horns of the Antelopes, Goats and Sheep are very apt to be pierced through and destroyed by insects. The reason is this : between the sheath and the core there is a great deal of blood and other matter. Few people take the trouble to take the horn off this core ; the matter putrefies, and the grubs are born, and speedily destroy the beauty of the specimen.

Unless you see the horns taken off with your own eyes do not believe that the Srinaggar *mochees* have done it.

When the horns have been loosened by the *mochees*, I invariably adopt the same plan. It has answered well; so I give it for the information of my readers who can try it or not, as they like.

Take off the horn and pour into it kerosine oil, taking care not to let the oil touch the outside of the horn, as it blackens it, and spoils the natural color. After the oil has remained in a few seconds, empty it out into another horn. Next with a saw cut off the top of the core ; it will be found to be composed of a cellular substance. Into these cells put plugs of wool or old cloth soaked in kerosine oil, or else in turpentine. Close the openings of the cells with wax if turpentine is employed. Round the core wrap some native cotton thread in order to make the sheath fit tightly, and with ordinary care the head should keep for ever. If it is intended to have the horn set up by an English taxidermist, doing anything more than cleaning the core is useless.

In some of the damper parts of India, where it is difficult to keep horns at all, it is advisable to varnish them, but not with any substance which would discolor them. I always use the most colorless spirit varnish I can get, and then dilute it with an equal bulk of turpentine. It evaporates, but can be put on yearly if necessary.

It is a mistake to polish a horn ; it spoils its value as a specimen ; you create a false impression of nature. A Bison's horns look pretty when polished, but amongst a collection it renders them out of place.

Never boil a skull; remove the flesh with a knife, then let maceration do the rest. It is a tedious business to clean the skull by letting it macerate in water, but it is the only way to make the bone look well.

Stag's head having solid horns are easily preserved. Nothing more is necessary than to remove all dirt and other matters from them. When obtained slightly covered with velvet, let them dry a little, rub in some kerosine oil, and set the velvet on fire with a match. It is a better plan than stripping off the velvet by hand. If the points have not set hard, it remains with the sportsman to settle whether they are worth keeping or not ; I should say decidedly not, unless as a memento of some very memorable stalk or drive.

Skins are easiest tanned if they have never been dried at all, but if the furrier lives at any distance, they must be dried, but never do so in the sun. If there is no shade available put up some blankets over them during the mid-day hours. If dried in the forests see that it is not done under a resinous fir, or at any rate that no resin touches the air.

Be very careful that all fatty matter is removed from Bear skins; once the fat has thoroughly soaked into the skin, the Indian dressers cannot remove it, and the skin remains hard and unpliant.

When Bear skins are sent in from a distance, more specially if in dry climate and a scorching sun, cover the fleshy side with birch bark or cloth. Of course wrap the skin up so that the hair is not injured.

Head skins are often troublesome to deal with. I have warned the lucky possesser of good speicmens to be sure and leave on plenty of the neck skin. This is more specially neces- sary in the case of Markhor, Oorial, Ther and maned or bearded animals in general. The eyes and lips require very careful skinning, and in hot climates arsenical soap, or some other preservative, is required. In cold climates, alum, well rubbed into the fleshy portions, is sufficient. Beware of wood ashes ; many a skin is spoilt by the coolies taking ashes from the fire before they have cooled down.

The Kashmir shikaris are too fond of overstretching the head skin by inserting a bow of willow wood to keep it from shrivelling up. The ends of this bow should be tied together with string, or the pressure exerted by the wood to regain its natural shape stretches the mouth and eye openings beyond remedy.

When skinning the head make the incision along the back of the neck, not below the chin.

If you really care for making a collection you cannot do better than buy Mr. Rowland Ward's treatise on these subjects.

I would sooner have one head of each variety of game artistically set up, and the remainder with simply the skull and horns than any number " stuffed ;" but it is very difficult to keep set-up heads in India from spoiling.

Why buy arsenical paste? You can make it very quickly, and for the merest trifle. Arsenic in very fine powder by weight, one part; soap cut into shreds and boiled, two parts, or more of the latter if a strong preparation is not required. Mix well, and just before it cools add a little turpentine, but not when *too hot*, or it will evaporate. Some people add camphor, but I do not see any use in doing this.

It is scarcely worth while to tan skins yourself; the furriers will, if they do not use salt, probably do it better and as cheap. Any really cared-for specimens should be at once sent to England.

In the plains, the teeth of Tigers or Leopards must be encased in wax, or they will split when exposed to the air and sun. This remark only applies to the hot and dry months.

CHAPTER XXVI.

Fishing in Kashmir— Tangrole and North-West generally.

I HAVE now come to the most difficult chapter to write. I have tried a great many of the smaller rivers with fly and with spoon-bait, with worms, and various other baits; but have never made much of it. The streams in the Nowboog valley hold plenty of the fish which are called by courtesy trout, but they will not take freely. At certain seasons of the year, all the small tributaries teem with fish, the Liddar and the Sindh being as good as any; but how to catch them in any quantity by means of rod, line, and hook I have never discovered.

In the Jhelum during June, July and August I have had some very fair fishing at Sumbul bridge. The fish take a small spoon freely. The best sport I had was in August. At this place I have not seen very large fish; the average caught with the spoon-bait are about 3lbs. weight. The largest do not exceed 8 to 10lbs.

Lower down the river at Ningbel where the Jhelum leaves the Woolar lake and passes out in the direction of Sopoor, very big mahseer are killed during the summer months. There is a famous run at Sopoor bridge and a fairly good one by the Baramulla fort. Below this again there is some grand looking water, but I have never heard of any large takes except at Sopoor and in the vicinity.

Below the Shukardin Ziarat, on the Woolar lake, will be seen a promontory composed of rock; near this fishing is to be had. Trolling from a boat is often successful, but the most killing bait is a frog. The frog should be tied on to the hook, and on the line at a distance of about eighteen inches from the bait a weight is fastened. The weight sinks to the bottom and keeps the frog down, but of course it has eighteen inches of play. This method of poaching is generally only employed at night.

In the various lakes the small fish can be speared from a boat, and on the Manasbal several fishermen are daily at work.

Every conceivable description of poaching is resorted to by the Kashmiris. Branches of streams are turned, and the wretched fish left high and dry. Unfortunately the villagers are too lazy to turn the water back again, and millions of young fry are destroyed.

Grass is thrown into the rivers in the winter; the fish get into the cover thus afforded them, and the fisherman spears

them with a long handled murderous looking weapon   Still
the rivers in the valley teem with fish ; the Woolar, Dal, and
other sheets of water afford refuges and safe breeding places.

With a fly composed of white feathers and a bit of crimson
cloth I have had fair sport on the summer evenings near many
of the Jhelum bridges.

On the Bhimber route there is good Mahseer fishing at
Nowshera. At Rajoori, four marches from Bhimber, Mahseer
up to 10lbs. in weight can be killed with grilse flies. The best
flies are red hackle with golden pheasant tip and bustard wing.

At the famous and well-known Tangrote, (Index Map) grand
sport is to be had. Tangrote is twenty-eight miles from
Jhelum, and, as many of my readers are aware, it is the spot
where the Poonch joins the Jhelum river. At Denah there is
a railway station which is only thirteen miles from Tangrote
bungalow. The return journey to Jhelum may be made by
boat and takes about seven hours. Within three hundred yards
of the fishing there is a good bungalow. This is in British
territory, but the fishing is done in Kashmir waters. In the
house, the tariff for boats is posted up ; moreover a fishing
register is kept, and shows the sport obtained for many years
back. The register goes a long way towards proving that
March and October are the best months in the year.

During heavy rain the Poonch comes down in flood, and no
fishing is to be obtained at Tangrote.

A friendly angler has kindly given the following information :—
" If the Poonch is muddy go to Kotli. This place is four marches
up the Poonch, and when that river is not fishable, sport may
be had in the tributary at Kotli. The fish in this small river
will take fly, and can be obtained up to 15lbs. in weight by this
method ; whilst on a spoon they are taken up to 40lbs."

For Tangrote waters I think I am correct in recommending
a four-inch gilt spoon to be used.

For a fishing outfit for the valley of Kashmir, I would take a
stiff trolling rod, big winch and a couple of lines, not less
than one hundred yards each. A light fly rod, a winch, and
a trout line, a hank of gut, gilt spoons, and a few small horn
baits. For flies, a few ordinary trout flies of almost any
description, some big white moths, and any grilse flies in which
bustard wing predominates.

In the mulberry season small fish are to be caught with this
fruit used as a bait, but it is very poor sport.

I cannot attempt to enumerate all the rivers in the North-
West and Punjab where I have patiently fished, and too often
with indifferent success, but mention the Giri in Nahun
territory ; the junction of the Asun river with the Jumna in
the Western Dun ; the junction of the Tonse river with the
Jumna below Kalsi in the same Dun. The Ganges and

Ramgunga are good in their seasons, but the best sport I have had was in the Sardah on the Nepaul frontier.

October is generally a good month, and so are February and March. Again when most of the snow water has cleared off in June I have secured some fish in the Jumna. For the Mandagni river, which is in the Rajah of Tiree's territory, the summer months are good.

Towards the Changchenmo, on the road between Tankse and the Marsemik, the small streams yield a few fish to the angler; but many more to the coolie, who catches them in his hands. The fish lie under the banks which are hollowed out by the scour, and are easily caught by the Kashmiris, who, as I before stated, are adepts at all poaching devices.